KINGDOM WARFARE

Prayer, Spiritual Warfare, and the Ministry of Angels

Jack W. Hayford
with
Mark Hayford

THOMAS NELSON PUBLISHERS
Nashville

CONTENTS

Kingdom Warfare: Prayer, Spiritual Warfare, and the Ministry of Angels is one of a series of study guides that focus exciting, discovery-geared coverage of Bible book and power themes—all prompting toward dynamic, Holy Spirit-filled living.

About the General Editor

JACK W. HAYFORD, noted pastor, teacher, writer, and composer, is the General Editor of the complete series, working with the publisher in the conceiving and developing of each of the books.

Dr. Hayford is Senior Pastor of The Church On The Way, the First Foursquare Church of Van Nuys, California. He and his wife, Anna, have four married children, all of whom are active in either pastoral ministry or vital church life. As General Editor of the *Spirit-Filled Life Bible,* Pastor Hayford led a four-year project, which has resulted in the availability of one of today's most practical and popular study Bibles. He is author of more than twenty books, including *A Passion for Fullness, The Beauty of Spiritual Language, Rebuilding the Real You,* and *Prayer Is Invading the Impossible.* His musical compositions number over four hundred songs, including the widely sung "Majesty."

About the Writer

MARK HAYFORD is pastor of the Foursquare Church in Glendale, California. He has pastored since his graduation from LIFE Bible College in 1983 and has also been active in missionary work throughout Scandinavia.

Mark is married to Diedre (nee Waterman), and he and DeeDee have three children: twin daughters, Jennifer and Jessica (9) and a son, Mark (4).

Of this contributor, the General Editor has remarked: "There is a special joy in seeing the maturation of your own offspring, coming to the place of becoming a proven source of blessing to many, many others. The user of this guide will, I believe, confirm my sense of the value Mark Hayford brings to assist in edifying study of God's Word."

THE KEYS
THAT KEEP ON FREEING

Is there anything that holds more mystery or more genuine practicality than a key? The mystery: "What does it fit? What can it turn on? What might it open? What new discovery could be made? The practicality: Something *will* most certainly open to the possessor! Something *will* absolutely be found to unlock and allow a possibility otherwise obstructed!

- Keys describe the instruments we use to access or ignite.
- Keys describe the concepts that unleash mind-boggling possibilities.
- Keys describe the different structures of musical notes which allow variation and range.

Jesus spoke of keys: "And I will give you the keys of the kingdom of heaven, and whatever you bind on earth will be bound in heaven, and whatever you loose on earth will be loosed in heaven" (Matt. 16:19).

While there is no conclusive list of exactly what keys Jesus was referring to, it is clear that He did confer upon His church—upon *all* who believe—the access to a realm of spiritual partnership with Him in the dominion of His kingdom. Faithful students of the Word of God, moving in the practical grace and biblical wisdom of Holy Spirit-filled living and ministry, have noted some of the primary themes which undergird this order of "spiritual partnership" Christ offers. The "keys" are *concepts*—biblical themes that are traceable through the Scriptures and verifiably dynamic when applied with soundly based faith under the lordship of Jesus Christ. The "partnership" is the *essential* feature of this release of divine grace;

(1) believers reaching to *receive* Christ's promise of "kingdom keys," (2) while choosing to *believe* in the Holy Spirit's readiness to actuate their unleashing, unlimited power today.

Companioned with the Bible book studies in the *Spirit-Filled Life Study Guide* series, the Kingdom Dynamic studies present a dozen different themes. This study series is an outgrowth of the Kingdom Dynamics themes included throughout the *Spirit-Filled Life Bible,* which provide a treasury of insight developed by some of today's most respected Christian leaders. From that beginning, studious writers have evolved the elaborated studies you'll pursue here.

The central goal of the subjects focused on in this present series of study guides is to relate "power points" of the Holy Spirit-filled life. Assisting you in your discoveries are a number of helpful features. Each study guide has twelve to fourteen lessons, each arranged so you can plumb the depths or skim the surface, depending upon your needs and interests. The study guides contain major lesson features, each marked by a symbol and heading for easy identification.

WORD WEALTH

The WORD WEALTH feature provides important definitions of key terms.

BEHIND THE SCENES

BEHIND THE SCENES supplies information about cultural beliefs and practices, doctrinal disputes, business trades, and the like that illuminate Bible passages and teachings.

AT A GLANCE

The AT A GLANCE feature uses maps and charts to identify places and simplify themes or positions.

 KINGDOM EXTRA

Because this study guide focuses on a theme of the Bible, you will find a KINGDOM EXTRA feature that guides you into Bible dictionaries, Bible encyclopedias, and other resources that will enable you to glean more from the Bible's wealth on the topic if you want something extra.

 PROBING THE DEPTHS

Another feature, PROBING THE DEPTHS, will explain controversial issues raised by particular lessons and cite Bible passages and other sources to which you can turn to help you come to your own conclusions.

 FAITH ALIVE

Finally, each lesson contains a FAITH ALIVE feature. Here the focus is, So what? Given what the Bible says, what does it mean for my life? How can it impact my day-to-day needs, hurts, relationships, concerns, and whatever else is important to me? FAITH ALIVE will help you see and apply the practical relevance of God's literary gift.

As you'll see, these guides supply space for you to answer the study and life-application questions and exercises. You may, however, want to record all your answers, or just the overflow from your study or application, in a separate notebook or journal. This would be especially helpful if you think you'll dig into the KINGDOM EXTRA features. Because the exercises in this feature are optional and can be expanded as far as you want to take them, we have not allowed writing space for them in this study guide. So you may want to have a notebook or journal handy for recording your discoveries while working through to this feature's riches.

The Bible study method used in this series revolves around four basic steps: observation, interpretation, correlation, and application. Observation answers the question, What does the text say? Interpretation deals with, What does the text mean?—not with what it means to you or me, but what it meant to its original readers. Correlation asks, What light do other Scripture passages shed on this text? And application, the goal of Bible study, poses the question, How should my life change in response to the Holy Spirit's teaching of this text?

If you have used a Bible much before, you know that it comes in a variety of translations and paraphrases. Although you can use any of them with profit as you work through the *Spirit-Filled Life Kingdom Dynamics Study Guide* series, when Bible passages or words are cited, you will find they are from the New King James Version of the Bible. Using this translation with this series will make your study easier, but it's certainly not necessary.

The only resources you need to complete and apply these study guides are a heart and mind open to the Holy Spirit, a prayerful attitude, and a pencil and a Bible. Of course, you may draw upon other sources, such as commentaries, dictionaries, encyclopedias, atlases, and concordances, and you'll even find some optional exercises that will guide you into these sources. But these are extras, not necessities. These study guides are comprehensive enough to give you all you need to gain a good, basic understanding of the Bible book being covered and how you can apply its themes and counsel to your life.

A word of warning, though. By itself, Bible study will not transform your life. It will not give you power, peace, joy, comfort, hope, and a number of other gifts God longs for you to unwrap and enjoy. Through Bible study, you will grow in your understanding of the Lord, His kingdom and your place in it, and those things are essential. But you need more. You need to rely on the Holy Spirit to guide your study and your application of the Bible's truths. He, Jesus promised, was sent to teach us "all things" (John 14:26; cf. 1 Cor. 2:13). So as you use this series to guide you through Scripture, bathe your study time in prayer, asking the Spirit of God to illuminate the text, enlighten your mind, humble your will, and comfort your heart. He will never let you down.

My prayer and goal for you is that as you unlock and begin to explore God's Book for living His way, the Holy Spirit will fill every fiber of your being to the joy and power God longs to give all His children. So read on. Be diligent. Stay open and submissive to Him. You will not be disappointed. He promises you!

Lesson 1/Discovering Prayer

"Come along, Jennifer, time to tuck you in and say your prayers."

"Jessica, it's your turn to say the blessing for dinner."

We may not have all grown up in homes where these words were spoken, but the picture of a small child with hands folded and head bowed is understood anywhere. Even in many homes where Jesus is seen as just a historical figure and God is only a questionable concept, prayers are said. Ask most anyone, and they will tell you that at one time or another they pray. It may be a "wish thrown to the man upstairs," an impassioned plea to "God, if You're there," or the simple recital of memorized lines, but we all pray.

While the practice of prayer is universal, there are very few people who seem to really understand prayer. The idea of invoking the Almighty to work because "I ask Him to" is an awesome thing. For most people, the belief that God will really answer that request is almost nonexistent. So why do people pray? They pray because "it might work," because "my grandmother swore by it," or, like anyone who ever just didn't know the right answer on a multiple choice test, "anything is better than nothing." So prayer has become the "anything" that gives us something to do rather than nothing. It is our "thing" to do when nothing *I* can do will help: "There is no hope, so I might as well give God a chance."

I know that these attitudes can seem almost blasphemous to those who believe in the power of prayer and have seen their prayers answered time and time again. However, we must remember that we become influenced by the world around us and, as a result, many Christians just don't see prayer as being much different from what is described above. We know that we should believe in prayer and that our prayers will be answered, but we just don't understand prayer in the first place. Why does an all-knowing God need me to tell Him my needs? Why does an all-Mighty God need my prayers in order to work? . . . What is prayer anyway?

To begin to answer these questions, look up the following scriptures in the Psalms and see if you can use them to form your own working definition of what prayer is. Here are some questions you can ask to help form this definition.

What word or words are used in place of the word *prayer*?

What is requested in the prayer? What truth is stated?

Does the attitude change at all in the prayer?

What picture of God is seen in the prayer?

What is the attitude of the one offering the prayer?

What is the prayer about?

Does the one offering the prayer indicate the reason for praying?

Ps. 17:1–9

Ps. 28:1–7

Ps. 55:16–23

Ps. 61:1–8

Ps. 102:1–22

Ps. 141

Ps. 142

WORD WEALTH

Pray, *proseuchomai.* The word is progressive. Starting with the noun, *euche,* which is a prayer to God that also includes making a vow, the word expands to the verb *euchomai,* a special term describing an invocation, request, or entreaty. Adding *pros,* "in the direction of" (God), *proseuchomai* becomes the most frequently used word for prayer in the New Testament.[1]

Prayer, *tephillah;* prayer, supplication, intercession. *Tephillah* occurs more than 75 times in the Old Testament, 32 of these in the Psalms. In 2 Chronicles 6:20, prayer from the temple in Jerusalem was afforded special significance, for day and night God watched over that house of prayer.[2] Today the house of prayer is to be a spiritual house built in our hearts (John 4:24).

Prayed, *palal.* To pray, entreat, intercede, make supplication. This verb occurs more than 80 times in the Old Testament. *Palal* speaks of prayer as intercession, asking someone with more power and wisdom to intervene on behalf of the one praying. For example, Hannah prayed for a son (1 Sam. 1:12); Hezekiah prayed for an extension of his life (Is. 38:2, 3); and Jonah prayed from within the fish's belly (Jon. 2:1–9). Furthermore, *palal* is found in the promise of 2 Chronicles 7:14, "If my people . . . will humble themselves, and pray . . . I will hear from heaven." See other intercessory examples of *palal* in Genesis 20:7, 17; Numbers 11:2; 1 Samuel 12:23.[3]

OUR CALL TO PRAY

There are many reasons to pray and many times when we need prayer. Search through the next passages with the topic of prayer in mind. See what reasons are given for prayer. Who taught us to pray? What benefits come as we pray? Are we commanded to pray? What places do humility and submission have in the reasons why we pray?

Luke 18:1–8

Luke 21:36

Eph. 6:18

James 4:3, 7, 8

1 Pet. 5:6, 7

 FAITH ALIVE

We all know we should pray, but why should we pray? What are the reasons behind our prayers? Do you find yourself just coming to God with a shopping list of things you would like Him to do? Are you seeking His will in your prayers? Are you getting to know Him better in your prayer times?

Think about these things, and be honest with yourself. Be conscious of these questions over the next few days and ask the Holy Spirit to help you see any patterns in your prayer life that should change. Then come back and answer these questions and ask the Lord to help you pray for the right reasons.

OPENING THE DOOR FOR GOD TO WORK

Prayer is the way that we are to submit everything to the Lord. As we pray, we invite God to come and work in the things that concern us. By obeying His command and placing our cares on Him, we are putting those things under His control rather than our own. This is not only submission, but the very act of humbling ourselves that 1 Peter 5:6, 7 speaks of. In prayer we are acknowledging that God can take care of all that concerns us and that we cannot. The open admission of our condition before the Lord is always needed as we approach His throne. The result is that God will exalt us in due time. Coming humbly before the Lord in prayer not only brings the exalting of our situation through answered prayer but also the exalting of our spirit into immediate communion with our Heavenly Father.

What are the things that we are to pray about as we submit things to the Lord in prayer? Who are we to pray for? When and how are we to pray? What other actions should accompany our prayers? Are there any results of the prayers noted? What are they? Look at the following scriptures and see what we are told.

2 Chr. 7:14

Ps. 32:5–7

Mark 14:38; Luke 22:32

1 Thess. 5:16–22

1 Tim. 2:1–3

James 5:13–16

KINGDOM EXTRA

With the help of a concordance or topical Bible, look to see what the prayers of various people in the Bible have been like. Here are a few of the people whose prayers you might want to find: Abraham, Moses, Solomon, Elijah, Jesus, Paul, Peter, David, Hannah, Daniel, Jehoshaphat, as well as many of the other kings, priests, prophets, and apostles in the Bible. Consider what attitudes are seen in their prayers and what responses God gave. What are the primary characteristics of these prayers? How is the heart of God seen in His response? How were the prayers generally spoken? What can we learn from these prayers?

FAITH ALIVE

Now that we have spent some time looking at the topic of prayer, did you learn anything new about prayer? Write down your own definition of prayer. How does this definition fit with your prayer life today? What is your concept of prayer? Is prayer healthy? boring? difficult? vibrant? What would you say to someone who asked, "Why do you pray? Why should I pray?" Is it valid to do something just because God said to do it? How does my submission to God allow Him to work in my life? Think about these things, and write down your feelings. Ask the Lord to help you gain His perspective on prayer and its place in your life. Let Him make your prayer times something to look forward to.

BEHIND THE SCENES

No people ever had a higher ideal of prayer than did the Jewish people, and no religion ever ranked prayer higher in the scale of priorities than did Judaism. But certain faults had crept into the Jewish habits of prayer. Please understand that these faults can and do occur anywhere. They are not the faults of neglect, but rather the faults of misguided devotion.

There were two rituals that every Jewish person was to perform daily: The *Shema* (prayerful quotation of Deut. 6:4–9; 11:13–21; Num. 15:37–41) to be recited at sunrise and sunset; and the *Shemoneh 'esreh* (eighteen set prayers to be quoted in order) to be prayed at the hours of prayer (9 A.M., noon and 3 P.M.).

Further, the Jewish liturgy supplied stated prayers for all occasions. There was hardly anything in life for which there was not a related formula prayer. There was prayer before and after each meal; there were prayers in connection with the rain and lightning, entering or leaving a city, seeing the new moon, using new furniture, and the list goes on.

The intent of this tradition was to incorporate God into every moment of the day. Yet as beautiful as these prayers are, there came a tendency for the faithful to recite words only out of duty without any sense of real communication with God. It is this mechanical praying that Jesus ultimately confronts in Matthew 6 as He speaks of those who say their prayers to appear good before other people.[4]

"Lord, Teach Us to Pray"

Hear the request of Jesus' disciples as they watch His life of prayer. After living daily with Jesus and learning so much at His feet, they come to Him with this desire, "Lord, teach us to pray" (Luke 11:1). This petition did not come from men who had no idea how to pray. This was the heart cry of those who see the powerful and life-begetting relationship that they have always longed for.

At the point where we become weary in praying, and even answers to our prayers don't bring fulfillment, there must be something more. It was this "something" that the disciples saw in the life of our Lord. They saw Someone who found complete fulfillment in a daily relationship with the heavenly Father. This is what the disciples longed for, and this is what we can find if we will learn how to pray from the example of Jesus.

To begin learning how to pray, look at Jesus' response to the disciples' request. The "Lord's Prayer," as it has been called, can be found in two locations in the Gospels. Read both of these texts with the surrounding verses and outline what is written there.

Matt. 6:5–15

Luke 11:1–14

AT A GLANCE

**PRAYER PRINCIPLES TAUGHT
IN THE LORD'S PRAYER[5]**

Matt. 6:8–13; Luke 11:2–4	Prayer Principles
"Our Father"	**1)** The Paternal Need: When you pray, all needs are met by the benevolence of a loving Father. This address to the Heavenly Father recognizes your relationship with Him. You must first come on the basis of a relationship secured for you in the atoning blood of Christ Jesus (Heb. 10:19–22; Gal. 4:4–6).
"Hallowed be Your Name"	**2)** God's Presence: Enter His presence through praise (Ps. 100:4). You have constant access to God's throne through praise and worship. Wherever you will praise Him, He will come and establish His rule (Ps. 22:3).
"Your Kingdom come. Your will be done"	**3)** God's Priorities: Declare that His kingdom priorities (Rom. 14:17) shall be established in yourself, your loved ones, your church, and your nation. God desires to rule in every situation that concerns us. As you set yourself

	to first seek His kingdom reign, you will find all that you need and more (Matt. 6:33).
"Give us"	**4)** <u>God's</u> <u>Provision</u>: Jesus the Need-Meeter told us to pray daily, asking Him to supply all our needs. God has already provided to meet our greatest need by sending Jesus to die for us. How much more can we expect Him to meet our daily needs from His vast storehouses of blessings (Phil. 4:19).
"And forgive us"	**5)** <u>God's</u> <u>Forgiveness</u>: We need God's forgiveness, and we need to forgive others. Daily set your will to walk in love and forgiveness. This step opens the door for a greater flow of God's grace in our lives, and the Lord will use this to bring freedom to others (John 20:23).
"Do not lead us into temptation . . . deliver us from the evil one."	**6)** <u>Power</u> <u>Over</u> <u>Satan</u>: Pray a hedge of protection about yourself and your loved ones (Job 1:9, 10; Ps. 91), and verbally put on the armor of God (Eph. 6:14–18). Seek to walk in righteousness, and the Lord will guide you (Ps. 37:23, 24). Resist the work of the enemy, and you will have victory (James 4:7).
"For Yours is the kingdom"	**7)** <u>Divine</u> <u>Partnership</u>: Praise God for sharing His kingdom, power, and glory with us (2 Tim. 4:18; Luke 10:19; John 17:22)! God daily calls us to partner in what He is doing. We can join in His plans by daily walking in open communication and relationship with Him.

 FAITH ALIVE

Now that you have completed this initial look at the biblical concept of prayer, take some time to record your insights.

What are your primary thoughts about prayer?

Are there any questions that this study has brought to your mind? Write them down so that you can come back to them further in the study as you find answers for them.

What do you hope to get from this study?

In what areas of your life (beliefs, moral standards and conduct, relationships, spiritual gifts, and the like) do you think this study will help you?

Is there anything that you have already found in your life that needs to be taken to God in prayer? List those items here so that you will remember to pray for them. You may also want to write down some of your feelings about these things in the form of a written prayer to the Lord.

1. *Spirit-Filled Life Bible* (Nashville, TN: Thomas Nelson Publishers, 1991), 1414, "Word Wealth: 6:6 pray."

2. Ibid., 618, "Word Wealth: 6:20 prayer."

3. Ibid., 747, "Word Wealth: 42:10 prayed."

4. William Barclay, *The Gospel of Mark, The Daily Bible Study Series* (Philadelphia, PA: The Westminster Press, 1975), 191–195.

5. *Spirit-Filled Life Bible*, 1414, chart based on "Kingdom Dynamics: 6:9–13 The Lord's Prayer."

Lesson 2/Intimacy with God

In my childhood home was an old army footlocker that served as the toy box for my sister, brother, and me. I remember this box well because of the many hours I must have spent searching through its contents or pestering someone to help me search for the one toy I "had to have." No other toy could take its place; I had to have "that one."

I don't know if it was the result of being the youngest of three children at the time or just a special heart for the underdog, but my favorite things to play with always seemed to be the smallest items in a box that was large enough to be my bed. Yet there I spent many hours searching and searching for the lost toy. I knew it could be found. I knew that finally my eyes would see through the layers of army men, broken crayons, building blocks, and miniature vehicles; there I would find what my child's heart sought.

The most important thing to me as a four-year-old child was to find that one toy. This toy was the center of my imaginary world, the figure that in my play represented my thoughts and virtues. This was the one for whom the building blocks were fashioned to make a home, the one who defended that home against incredibly superior numbers of "bad army men." This was my favorite, and all the work of my childhood world had to halt until I found him; and, sooner or later, I always did.

"Seek and you will find" (Matt. 7:7). This is not just the story of a four-year-old child; these are the words of Jesus that answer to the needs of a race who have lost the most important thing to them—a relationship with God. We need this relationship. It is the most vital thing we can obtain. It is the only reason worth living for, because He is the center of our world (Col. 1:16, 17). Yet sadly, most of us are often too easily satisfied with a substitute. We settle for something less than true intimacy with God.

Like a child searches for a prized object, we are to set ourselves to seek the living God. Where will we find Him? How must we search? What will happen to those who seek Him? to those who don't? Read through the following scriptures and see if you can answer these questions. Also, be looking for other things you should seek as well as key words about what your heart and attitude should be like as you seek God.

Deut. 4:27–31

2 Chr. 7:14

Ps. 9:10

Ps. 69:30–34

Is. 65:10–15

Jer. 29:11–13

WORD WEALTH

Seek, *baqash.* To seek, to diligently look for, to search earnestly until the object of the search is located. *Baqash* can apply to seeking a person, a particular item, or a goal (such as seeking to destroy a city, 2 Sam. 20:19). *Baqash* occurs more than 210 times in the Old Testament.[1]

Know, *yada.* To know, to perceive, to distinguish, to recognize, to acknowledge, to be acquainted with; to "know intimately," that is, sexually; also to acknowledge, recognize, esteem, and endorse.[2] This is the same word used in Proverbs 3:6: "In all your ways <u>acknowledge</u> Him." This is a call to daily grow into an intimate and life-begetting relationship with God.

A DREADFUL THOUGHT

From Hosea 5:6 comes this terrible phrase: "They shall go to seek the LORD, but they will not find *Him*." This scripture is a picture of what can happen to people who do not prepare themselves to seek the Lord, but rather come to God "their own way." God calls us to come by a way that He has prepared for us. God never comes to meet us on our terms but makes clear later in the same passage that His withdrawal from these people is until they acknowledge their sin.

Read Hosea 5 and note the things that are happening or will happen because of the sins of God's people. Write down also any particular sins that are noted and what must take place for the sinners to find God.

FAITH ALIVE

Jesus says that we need to become like children to see His kingdom—openhearted and honestly searching without being held back by our pride. It is our pride that prevents us from fully pursuing things God's way. Doesn't it sound foolish to say, "I think my way is better than God's." We know that God's wisdom is far greater than our own, yet each time we fail to do things His way and insist on our own methods, we are living out that same statement.

It is this pride that so often keeps us from living in all that He has provided for us. Spend some time asking yourself the following questions, and then write down and pray about any matters of pride that you may need the Lord to work on in your life.

Are you at times embarrassed by your faith? proud?

Is it hard for you to show your emotions to God in times of praise or prayer? in public? in private?

Is open, verbal praise or prayer hard for you?

Do you find yourself trying to "manage" things on your own rather than surrendering to God's way or depending on His promises—alone?

EXPRESSING YOUR HEART TO GOD

One of the most important parts of any relationship is honest and open communication. This is no different when it comes to our relationship with our Heavenly Father. We need open and honest communication with Him. This communication will not break down on His side. We are the ones who tend toward hiding our hearts from others.

As you work through this next section, keep your focus on communication with God. See what you learn about this from both sides, His tendencies as well as ours. In each case ask yourself what pictures you see that you should emulate in your relationship with the Lord. What is God's tendency toward open communication with us in these passages? Who initiates it? Is anything held back?

Gen. 18:17–21

Ex. 3:1–22

1 Sam. 3:1–14

How does communication begin in these passages? What is the purpose? How is the heart of each person seen? What physical and verbal expression is there?

Ps. 63

Ps. 138

Luke 22:41–44

A TRULY SATISFYING RELATIONSHIP

Jesus was being urged by His disciples to eat when He responded with the words, "I have food to eat of which you do not know"(John 4:32–34). The disciples were perplexed and wondered if Jesus had managed to get some food elsewhere without their knowing it. Jesus then made clear that His satisfaction and strength came from His relationship and partnership with the Heavenly Father.

This was not a discourse to rebuke the disciples for fulfilling basic needs of the physical body. This was Jesus' call to look for a greater fulfillment that would be daily strength just as food is for our bodies. Our relationship with God is meant to provide this kind of fullness and strength, but it only comes as we really start to know God. Jesus knew the Father well — well enough to know that He was doing His will.

What do the following scriptures have to say about knowing God?

Ps. 34:8–18

Prov. 3:5, 6

Jer. 9:23, 24

Matt. 11:27–30

FAITH ALIVE

Now that you have had some time to look into developing an intimate relationship with the Heavenly Father, think about what you have learned. What concepts have been made alive or seem to be new to you? Do you feel as if you understand them? Take time to ask for understanding.

How could you plan to incorporate these truths into your life? What things might you do to help cultivate your relationship with God?

FINDING THE ULTIMATE IN INTIMACY

When Jesus prays for us in John 17:20–26, He asks the Father that we would have the most intimate of relationships with Him. Then He points the way. Jesus prays that His followers would be "one in Us" (referring to the Godhead, v. 21). This is a prayer for unity among all believers in conjunction with God. Many scriptures give a picture of the power and beauty of unity among God's children and with Him. Where this unity exists we find special displays of God's power, presence, and purpose. It seems that Jesus Himself shows that intimacy with the Father begins with love for one another.

Read John 17:20–26 and see what Jesus says about unity in His body.

What is Jesus' opening request about being "one"?

What is mentioned about the results of our unity?

What has Jesus done to allow us to be one?

In the following scriptures you can learn more about the incredible power released as we pray and live in unity in the body of Christ. Look through them and record what they say about God's power, presence, and purpose in a united church.

2 Chr. 5:13, 14

Ps. 133:1–3

Acts 2:1–4

2 Cor. 11:2; Rev. 21:2, 3, 9

WORD WEALTH

One, *'echad*. One, a unit; united; unity. *'Echad* comes from the root *'achad,* "to bring together, to unify; to collect one's thoughts." *'Echad* serves to portray the same range of meaning as "one" does in English, from the very narrowest sense (one and one only, as in Eccl. 9:18, "one sinner destroys much good") to the broadest sense (one made up of many, as in Gen. 2:24, where a man and his wife "shall become one flesh").[3] *'Echad* is considered one of the most important words in the Old Testament, as it is used to describe God as one (Deut. 6:4).

With one accord, *homothumadon.* Being unanimous, having mutual consent, being in agreement, having group unity, having one mind and purpose. The disciples had an intellectual unanimity, an emotional rapport, and volitional agreement in the newly founded church. In each of its occurrences *homothumadon* shows a harmony leading to action.[4]

FAITH ALIVE

Take a moment to review this lesson and collect your thoughts regarding the pursuit of an intimate prayer relationship with God. What is it? List the attributes as well as the definition (John 12).

To your view, what would you think is the hardest aspect of building this relationship? How could you plan to overcome those difficulties?

Do you think unity with the body of Christ is important to your developing personal intimacy with God? Why?

What steps could you take to grow together with God's family?

Take some time to pray over the actions that you plan to take. Ask the Lord for His wisdom in developing and implementing plans to grow closer to Him and His people.

1. *Spirit-Filled Life Bible* (Nashville, TN: Thomas Nelson Publishers, 1991), 1264, "Word Wealth: 5:15 seek."

2. Ibid., 87, "Word Wealth: 3:7 know."

3. Ibid., 263, "Word Wealth: 6:4 one."

4. Ibid., 1624, "Word Wealth: 2:1 with one accord."

Lesson 3/Bringing Our Needs

The longer I'm a father, the more I love the fact that God calls Himself our "Heavenly Father"!

I love to tell people that because it is so true. As I raise my children, I am learning more and more what the heart of God is toward us. I see how He loves, nurtures, teaches, comforts, and directs His children. He is patient, caring, tender, sharing, and in every way loving toward us.

I know also that there are times He is sad because His children don't trust Him and choose to ignore His fatherly wisdom. There are times when He is grieved by our disobedience. He must at times let us learn the error of our ways and let us stumble because we wouldn't let Him hold our hands. And there are times when He must chastise us so that we will learn the way we should go.

All of these things are the work of a father. It is not just the fact of His giving us life that makes God our Heavenly Father, but it is also the fact that He raises us as His children. Any parent knows that begetting children is the easiest part; helping them grow up is the primary work. So the work of our salvation—being birthed into the family of God—is one that progresses as we mature in our life with the Lord. There are no areas of our lives where our Father will not desire to participate. God is there when we are working, sleeping, eating, playing—anything we do, He is there.

The heart of any father is to care for his children this way. Jesus noted that even with our sinful ways we still know how to give good things to our children (Matt. 7:11). He mentioned the giving nature of an earthly father to show us how our Heavenly Father desires to give to us also, "above all that we ask or think" (Eph. 3:20; Phil. 4:19).

This is what the Heavenly Father is like—wanting to give to His children. Yet He says we still need to ask. "You do not have because you do not ask" (James 4:2). The Bible often directs us to ask. Read the following passages and see what they have to say about asking:

How are we to ask? (In what name, attitude, state of expectancy, and so on?)

What should we ask for?

How are we *not* to ask?

Why are *you* to ask?

What will happen when you ask?

Luke 11:9–13

John 14:13, 14

John 16:23–27

James 1:5–8

James 4:2, 3

1 John 3:18–23

1 John 5:14, 15

 FAITH ALIVE

Now that you have taken a look at how the heart of our Father is disposed to meet and satisfy our needs, take time to reflect on how you have viewed God's heart toward you in the past. Have you seen prayer as trying to convince Him to work? Has your aim been to prove yourself to Him in order to get answers? Have you thought that He only answered prayers if you did the right things to "make Him answer?" Define below exactly how you have inclined to view God's heart toward you.

List areas where you recognize your need to let God's love become more real to you. Take this list to the Lord in prayer and let Him work on those things in your life.

A LESSON IN HUMILITY

Whenever we come to the Lord, the condition of our heart is of utmost importance. We must have a heart that acknowledges *who* God is and *what* He is like (Heb. 11:6). We must also have a heart that recognizes God's abilities to meet our needs. It is this understanding of His greatness contrasted with our own insufficiency that humbles us before His throne.

Coming to God with humility is an absolute imperative. Still, too many have confusing ideas of what humility really is. We live in a world that thinks of humility as some order of a "see yourself as a worm" proposition. This is in no wise the case. True humility has everything to do with a person of power in the Kingdom of God and nothing to do with being ashamed of who God has made you to be. When our sinful shame is forgiven through Christ, God's view of us is as *treasured ones.* Examine how these verses describe God's view of you as His own: Malachi 3:17, 18; Ephesians 2:4–6; 1 Peter 2:9, 10.

Humility is living your life according to these truths—the truth about your sinless estate in Christ, yet your flaws as a human; the truth about God's mightiness and His tender grace; the truth about others and their needs; all of these things weighed in prayer lend toward humility, and thereby relate to how we come to the Father in prayer.

Your approach to the Lord should mirror the following points of understanding. Can you think of scriptures which support these points?

1) God's ways are greater than mine, so I will live in submission to His word and will.

2) God cares about and will meet my needs, so I will bring them humbly to Him.

3) God loves this world, so I will be His instrument to reach others through my prayers.

Read the following passages to better understand how to humble yourself before God. Note the things that others have done or the things you are directed to do to be humble before the Lord. What are the things listed to do? What will happen if you do these things? What examples of humility do you see? What did those people do to show humility or to humble themselves? What was the final result seen in their lives?

2 Chr. 32:24–26

2 Chr. 12:1–9

Ps. 35:13, 14

Matt. 18:3, 4

Acts 20:17–24

Phil. 2:3, 4; 5–11

1 Pet. 5:1–7

WORD WEALTH

Humility, *einophrosune.* Modesty, lowliness, humble-mindedness, a sense of moral insignificance, and a humble attitude of unselfish concern for the welfare of others. It is a total absence of arrogance, conceit, and haughtiness. The word is a combination of *tapeinos* (see below), "humble," and *phren,* "mind." The word was unknown in classical nonbiblical Greek. Only by abstaining from self-aggrandizement can members of the body of Christ maintain unity and harmony.[1]

Humbles, *tapeinoo.* Literally, "to make low," used of a mountain in Luke 3:5. Metaphorically, the word means to debase, humble, lower oneself. It describes a person who is devoid of all arrogance and self-exaltation—a person who is willingly submitted to God and His will.[2]

Humble, *shaphel.* To make low, depress, sink, lower, debase, humble, abase. *Shaphel* occurs twenty-nine times in the Old Testament and is generally translated "humble," "bring down," or "make low." Notice the irony of Proverbs 29:23, "A man's pride will bring him low, but the humble in spirit will retain honor."[3]

PRAYING BOLDLY IN FAITH

It can seem to us contradictory to come both in humility and boldness, but that is exactly how the Lord would have us to come. How can the two of these work together? The key is absolute, dependent *faith in God!*

Faith in our own plans or strength only promotes prideful self-dependence, but faith in God's wisdom and power encourages us to come boldly to Him, *expecting* to receive from Him while *focusing* on our need of Him. This causes humility to grow in us.

See what you can learn of faith in James 1:5–7; 2:14–26 and Hebrews 11:1—12:2. Note what you are learning about faith, both positive (what you should do) and negative (what you should not do).

James 1:5–7; 2:14–26

Heb. 11:1—12:2

 AT A GLANCE

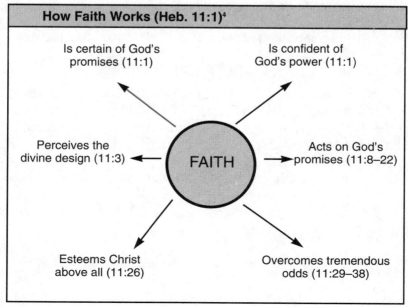

How Faith Works (Heb. 11:1)[4]

Is certain of God's promises (11:1)

Is confident of God's power (11:1)

Perceives the divine design (11:3) ←

FAITH

→ Acts on God's promises (11:8–22)

Esteems Christ above all (11:26)

Overcomes tremendous odds (11:29–38)

WORD WEALTH

Faith, *pistis.* Conviction, confidence, trust, belief, reliance, trustworthiness, and persuasion. In the New Testament setting, *pistis* is the divinely implanted principle of inward confidence, assurance, trust, and reliance in God and all that He says. The word sometimes denotes the object or the content of belief (Acts 6:7; 14:22; Gal. 1:23).[5]

Boldness, *parrhesia.* Outspokenness, unreserved utterance, freedom of speech, with frankness, candor, cheerful courage, and the opposite of cowardice, timidity, or fear. *Parrhesia* is not a human quality but a result of being filled with the Holy Spirit.[6]

Doubting nothing, *diakrino.* Has two definitions: 1) To judge thoroughly; to decide between two or more choices; to make a distinction; to separate two components, elements, or factors; to render a decision; to evaluate carefully. 2) The word also connotes a conflict with oneself, in the sense of hesitating, having misgivings, doubting, being divided in decision making, or wavering between hope and fear.[7]

Believe, *pisteuo.* The verb form of *pistis* (see above), "faith." It means to trust in, have faith in, be fully convinced of, acknowledge, rely on. *Pisteuo* is more than credence in church doctrines or articles of faith. It expresses reliance upon and a personal trust that produces obedience. It includes submission and positive confession of the lordship of Jesus.[8]

JESUS TEACHES FAITH

Now that you have taken a look at coming to the Lord boldly with faith and a humble heart, look over what Jesus said about faith as He ministered daily to the needs of people. Hear His words to His disciples as He taught them the power and importance of faith.

As you study Jesus' words, answer these questions below:

For what things can we have faith? Why? How much faith do we need?

What pictures does Jesus use to illustrate great faith?

In whom are you to have faith?

What is the result of our faith?

What leads to faith?

What is Jesus' heart toward those who don't have faith?

Matt. 9:22–29

Mark 10:27

Mark 11:22–26

Mark 16:17, 18

Luke 7:1–10

John 12:44–47

FAITH ALIVE

What new attitudes or emotions have been stirred up in your heart through this lesson that you want to bring to the Lord in prayer? As you write them down, name each one, putting it on your lips before the Lord, believing He will answer your prayer.

1. *Spirit-Filled Life Bible* (Nashville, TN: Thomas Nelson Publishers, 1991), 1666, "Word Wealth: 20:19 humility."

2. Ibid., 1439, "Word Wealth: 18:4 humbles."

3. Ibid., 1077, "Word Wealth: 13:18 humble."

4. *The Wesley Bible* (Nashville, TN: Thomas Nelson Publishers, 1990), 1858, "Chart: How Faith Works (Heb. 11:1)."

5. *Spirit-Filled Life Bible*, 1492, "Word Wealth: 11:22 faith."

6. Ibid., 1632, "Word Wealth: 4:31 boldness."

7. Ibid., 1646, "Word Wealth: 11:12 doubting nothing."

8. Ibid., 1704, "Word Wealth: 10:9 believe."

Lesson 4/The Power of Purity

"Keep your heart with all diligence, for out of it *spring* the issues of life" (Prov. 4:23).

Our hearts are the center of our physical beings. Without the work of this organ, life is impossible. It provides a constant supply of blood to every part of the body. So, in the simplest and essentially beginning way, this proverb is a good reminder to care for the physical condition of your heart. Of course, the writer's objective is to caution the wise with the reminder: "The *internal* you—your 'heart of hearts' requires the utmost care, spiritually!"

Caring for your physical heart is of the most basic practical wisdom. Doctors regularly warn us to watch our intake of foods that contain cholesterol. This is because cholesterol—tiny globules of fatty-building potential—can build up layer upon layer in the veins and eventually stop the flow of blood throughout the body. It makes the heart's work harder to do, and eventually even ordinary work and can lead to a heart failure.

There is similar danger in our spiritual life if we do not keep a watch on our hearts. Sin, like cholesterol, slows down the flow of God's grace in our life (the cleansing blood of Jesus). The inevitable result, unattended, will be the slowing our heartbeat for holiness and the "loss of a heart for God." The redemptive, <u>daily</u> flow of Christ's cleansing work, "through blood," is as vital to our spiritual life as our bodies' blood is to our physical life. Without it we waste away—loss of spiritual vitality becoming certain and destructive.

Just as doctors prescribe special diets for patients with heart problems, God has provided dietary instructions for us, because it is in the fallen nature of man to have a propensity for "heart trouble" (our struggles with temptation and sin).

To prepare the way—and sustain a heart for prayer power, let's study the keys to personal purity of heart. A heart kept in purity will be a heart prepared for power prayer! Read through the following passages to discover God's diet for the health of your heart. Write down the things that you are to do to keep your heart clean.

Ps. 119:9–16

Prov. 16:5–9

John 13:8

Acts 2:42, 47

1 Cor. 6:9–11

Phil. 4:8

Heb. 9:11–15

2 Pet. 1:5–10; 3:1, 2

 FAITH ALIVE

Look over the list that you have written of things that help keep your heart clean. Which of these do you feel need practical application in your daily life?

How do you view your present response and practice in living within the wisdom of these truths? Write your thoughts on this.

THE PATHWAY TO PURITY

It is fine to give a diet to someone who is at risk for heart failure, but you need more than a diet for a person in the throes of a heart attack. As important as a *daily* diet for living purely is, there must also be a course of action to take when you find that your heart is already functioning far below the optimum or, worse, in crisis.

Second Timothy 2:22 gives a clear plan for restoring and living in purity. Use the supplemental texts and "Word Wealth" features below to help you outline this path.

What is the first thing this verse instructs us to do?

Look at "lusts" in "Word Wealth" (p. 45) and examine James 1:15, noting what can result if you do not flee?

Study Acts 8:21, 22 and 1 John 1:9; 2:1, 2. How should you respond if your heart is already wrong before God? What does *repentance* mean here? What does Jesus do when we sin?

After you flee "lusts," what four things are you to pursue?

Look up the following scripture, thinking each through in the light of the "Word Wealth" definition of each key word. Then record how each of these qualities can help keep us from sin.

Righteousness (Prov. 11:3–6)

Love (1 John 3:1–3; 5:2, 3)

Faith (Rom. 1:16, 17; 5:1, 2)

Peace (Rom. 14:18, 19; Matt. 5:9)

 WORD WEALTH

Advocate, *parakletos.* From *para,* "beside," and *kaleo,* "to call," hence, allied to one's side. The word signifies an intercessor, comforter, helper, advocate, counselor. In non-biblical literature *parakletos* had the technical meaning of an attorney who appears in court in another's behalf.[1] In 1 John 2:1 Jesus is seen as standing on our behalf and in our place before the throne of God that His blood would be accounted as payment for our sin.

Repent, *metanoeo.* From *meta,* "after," and *noeo,* "to think." Repentance is a decision that results in a change of mind, which in turn leads to a change of purpose and action.[2]

Lusts, *epithumia.* A strong desire, an intense craving for something. It can be used for both good and evil desires. . . . Most usage of this word, however, is negative, such as gratifying sensual cravings, desiring the forbidden, and striving for things, persons, or experiences contrary to the will of God.[3]

Righteousness, *diakaiosune.* Just, the quality of being right. Broadly, the word suggests conformity to the revealed will of God in all respects. *Diakaiosune* is both judicial and gracious. God declares the believer righteous, in the sense of acquitting him, and imparts righteousness to him (2 Cor. 5:21).[4]

Faith, *pistis.* Conviction, confidence, trust, belief, reliance, trustworthiness, and persuasion. In the New Testament setting, *pistis* is the divinely implanted principle of inward confidence, assurance, trust, and reliance in God and all that He says.[5]

Love, *agape.* A word to which Christianity gave new meaning. Outside of the New Testament it rarely exists in Greek manuscripts of the period. *Agape* denotes an undefeatable benevolence and unconquerable goodwill that always seeks the highest goodwill of the other person, no matter what he does. It is the self-giving love that gives freely without asking anything in return and does not consider the worth of its object. *Agape* is more a love by choice than *philos,* which is a love by chance; and it refers to the will rather than the emotion. *Agape* describes the unconditional love that God has for the world.[6]

Peace, *eirene.* A state of rest, quietness, and calmness; an absence of strife; tranquility. It generally denotes a perfect well-being. *Eirene* includes harmonious relationships between God and men, men and men, nations, and families. Jesus as Prince of Peace gives peace to those [who live under His lordship].[7]

THE PATHWAY TO PURITY CONTINUED

You have already looked into the call to repentance and the pursuit of a godly life-style. Continue meditating on 2 Timothy 2:22 and see what other steps are needed in the pathway to purity. Below you will find texts and questions to direct this study.

Should you pursue righteousness, faith, love, and peace apart from other people? If not, with whom should you join?

In James 5:13–16 how does living within a fellowship of believers bring health and purity? What part does confession play in this?

From 1 John 1:5–10 explain how living in the family of God—"fellowship together"—helps expose and cleanse our sins. What does it say about people who don't confess their sin? What happens when you confess your sins?

 PROBING THE DEPTHS

The questions surrounding confession are baffling to many. Among various church groups the doctrine regarding confession varies widely. See what you can learn by looking up "confession" in a Bible dictionary or encyclopedia. For deeper study use a concordance or topical Bible to find all of the ways that confession is made in the Bible. Use this study to determine the place, value, and method of confession that should be implemented in your life.

A PASSION FOR PURITY

In Psalm 51 we find the prayer of a heart crying out to God for restored purity. Read this passage and note what you see of the following:

1. Confession

2. Repentance

3. Cleansing

4. Restoration

What does the psalmist say are true "sacrifices" to God?

What does the psalmist ask of God?

 BEHIND THE SCENES

Psalm 51 was written as David cried for mercy from God after he had committed adultery and subsequently murder to hide his sexual sinning (2 Sam. 11:1—12:23). This story clearly shows God's love in that He sends Nathan the prophet to confront and restore David into right relationship with Him. At the same time the righteousness of God is underlined in His refusal to allow His servant David to walk in unconfessed sin.

Throughout this Psalm there are truths about God's nature and character that are rarely seen clearly by those who do not have a personal, intimate relationship with Him. God's mercy, lovingkindness, righteousness, and true desires are a few of these attributes.

THE LIFE OF THE RIGHTEOUS

A righteous man has much to look forward to, but there is a life-style that he must live in order to enjoy the benefits. A pure, daily walk with the Lord blesses you as well as those around you. Search the following scriptures to help you see the characteristics of this fulfilling life. Record both the blessings on and actions of the righteous, upright, or pure of heart. Contrast these things with what is seen in the life of the wicked and ungodly. What does God do for the righteous? for the wicked? Where do the righteous live? How do they come to God? Do the wicked dwell there also? Can they come to God the same way?

Ps. 1:1–6

Ps. 15:1–5

Prov. 10:2–7, 20–32

Prov. 11:3–11, 18–23

 FAITH ALIVE

What is the most notable thing that you have learned in this lesson?

Why do you think this point stands out to you?

In what area do you think this lesson will have the greatest impact on your life? Why? What do you think the result will be?

How do you see the righteousness of God in your life? Is it growing daily? Why do you think this is so?

Do you desire to see greater purity in your life? Write a letter to God expressing your desire to live in purity. Include things that you see His needing to help you with, such as bad habits, thoughts, desires, and so on. Pray over these things, asking the Lord to create a clean heart in you just as David asked in Psalm 51.

1. *Spirit-Filled Life Bible* (Nashville, TN: Thomas Nelson Publishers, 1991), 1605, "Word Wealth: 15:26 Helper."

2. Ibid., 1407, "Word Wealth: 3:2 repent."

3. Ibid., 1855, "Word Weatlh: 2:22 lusts."

4. Ibid., 1857, "Word Wealth: 4:8 righteousness."

5. Ibid., 1492, "Word Wealth: 11:22 faith."

6. Ibid., 1694, "Word Wealth: 5:5 love."

7. Ibid., 1510, "Word Wealth: 1:79 peace."

Lesson 5/Faithful in Prayer

"Sons, never start to climb a mountain unless you are going to the top."

Oh, how I remember those words that my father spoke to my brother and me! That great statement speaks such truth about being a person of virtue, endurance, commitment, and faithfulness—a person who first measures and then prepares accordingly for a challenge before he sets out. In thinking of our becoming faithful in prayer, I remember my dad's words because he seemed so serious when he spoke them; and when my dad was serious, we kids listened. Similarly, it's wise for us to hear the Heavenly Father's call to faithful prayer. Look up the following verses, and note what the rewards of "seeking" God faithfully—of "asking" God greatly—can be:

Ps. 2:8

Jer. 33:3

John 14:12–14

It's a curious fact that it was years after the time my dad made his "mountain-climbing" statement that I realized his remark—intended to be sincere—was strange at the time, because immediately following his words, he announced that we were abandoning our climb halfway up the "hill" we were on. But that was due to an issue of perspective. I was only about 5 years old at the time, and we were standing on a plateau, having just climbed a rather steep portion of terrain (which, to a young boy, was a mountain in itself). But now we moved from there and prepared to start up another nearby hill that was a *real* "mountain" and challenge. It had seemed to me we had left one "mountain" and gone on to another, when, in fact, the change had merely occurred at the time we were midway in one extended climb. This issue of perspective—thinking we're at the peak when, in fact, we've just begun—can keep us from reaching the heights of potential God has for us in our spiritual lives. It's not that we couldn't reach the top if we continued to climb. We're just too inclined to stop because we think we've arrived. Like I, who as a little child, thought one short portion of the climb was the whole mountain, any of us can too readily stop climbing when we're still far short of the heights—never having seen the vistas that the Lord has waiting for us.

So, just as with mountain climbing, let's not stop pursuing prayer until we have reached what we've set out to attain. In prayer, that "setting out" is a commitment to seeing God's will penetrate and prevail in specific, given situations. That's the ultimate peak.

Faithfulness is more than just perseverance; it requires a person to be full of faith in a way that begets life rather than manifesting in dead unproductivity (James 2:14–26). Jesus taught faithfulness in several ways. Look at these scriptures and see what you can learn about the characteristics of faithfulness. The questions asked with each passage are to help trigger thought and response.

Luke 14:27–32: What part does preparation have in faithfulness? Is faithfulness possible without it? Why?

Matt. 7:24–27: What is the difference between believing and living out what you believe? What does faithfulness build into your life? How?

Luke 16:10–12: What is the true test of faithfulness? Who can be trusted with great things? Can a person be faithful in some things and not in others? Why not?

Matt. 25:1–30: How do the teachings of these parables compare to the previous texts mentioned above? What did the wise virgins do that set them apart? How was the unprofitable servant faithless in his task?

You can see that faithfulness requires preparation and thoughtful action as well as consistency. These are features that should be incorporated into your prayer life. Jesus also taught on one other aspect of faithfulness in prayer. Look at Luke 11:5–13 and 18:1–8 to see what Jesus says about boldness and steadfastness to purpose.

What pictures does Jesus give of prayer?

Luke 11

Luke 18

How do these reflect boldness and steadfastness for purpose?

Luke 11

Luke 18

What does Jesus say will be God's answer to prayer if we
continue?

Luke 11

Luke 18

PROBING THE DEPTHS

Does God answer our prayers because we keep asking? Does He refuse to answer because our continual asking
shows a lack of faith? Both of these questions have been
bantered about by Bible teachers over the years, with some
standing clearly on each side, and others insisting that there
are times to stand in faith and times to pursue in warfare.

Below are a number of scriptures that provide teaching
and examples on this subject. As you read through these, ask
the Holy Spirit to help you understand what is being taught:
Genesis 18:23–32; Joshua 10:12–14; 1 Kings 18:22–38, 41–44;
2 Kings 13:15–19; Matthew 6:7, 8; Mark 11:22–24; Luke 7:2–10;
2 Corinthians 12:8–10; Ephesians 6:18; James 1:5–8.

After reading these scriptures you may find that you still
have questions left unanswered. Here are some books you
may want to read on the subject of prayer that will help
answer these questions:

Prayer Is Invading the Impossible, by Jack W. Hayford (Ballantine, 1983)

Prayer: Key to Revival, by Paul Y. Cho and R. Whitney Manzano (Word, Inc., 1987)

With Christ in the School of Prayer, by Andrew Murray (Zondervan, 1983)

Prayer and Praying Men, by Edward M. Bounds (Baker Books, 1992)

Understand that the view you hold on this subject is not to divide you from others in the body of Christ, but rather, it is for the strengthening of your personal prayer life through understanding God's Word.

 FAITH ALIVE

Describe the traits in your life that indicate faithfulness.

What traits would you like to see in the future? What makes these important to you?

In what area of your life do you show the most faithfulness (for example, friendship, career, finances, spiritual growth, and so on)? What makes that area seem to be stronger than others?

In what area of your life do you show the least faithfulness? Why do you think this is true?

How do you think you can grow in faithfulness? What steps will you take to do this?

 ## BEHIND THE SCENES

The entire course of western civilization has been greatly influenced by ancient Greece. This is especially true of western thought and philosophy and can be seen clearly in the contrast between the Greek and Hebrew concept of knowledge.

To the Greek way of thinking, knowledge had only to do with mental recognition. If a person had studied a subject and knew the facts, then he was considered to "know" that subject.

The Hebrew idea of knowledge included practical application and experience. Simple study and mental storage of information was not "knowing." The living practice of the things learned was required to "know" a subject.

It will help any Christian to understand that the thought behind New Testament writings is essentially Hebrew, although it was written in Greek as that was the common language of the day. The biblical concept of "knowing" involves *experience,* not merely *exposure* to the truth or to a set of facts.

FAITH IS 99% FAITHFULNESS

The biggest part of our faith-walk with Jesus is living a life ~~f~~ithfulness. Often we concentrate so heavily on having faith that we fail to recognize faithfulness as being a life that "lives in" rather than "strives for" faith.

One of the most often quoted statements on faith is a New Testament quotation from an Old Testament verse. Using the "Word Wealth" section below, compare Habakkuk 2:2–4 with Hebrews 10:36–38 and answer the following questions:

How are "faith," "faithfulness," "endurance," and "waiting" related in these passages?

For what do we need endurance? (Also see James 1:12.)

Who will receive the promises God has given here? What are the attributes of those who will not receive?

How do the two definitions of faith below show the need for steadfastness?

WORD WEALTH

Faith, *pistis.* Conviction, confidence, trust, belief, reliance, trustworthiness, and persuasion. In the New Testament setting, *pistis* is the divinely implanted principle of inward confidence, assurance, trust, and reliance in God and all that He says.[1]

Shall live, *chayah.* To live, to stay alive, be preserved; to flourish, to enjoy life; to live in happiness; to breathe, be alive, be animated, recover health, live continuously. The fundamental idea is "to live and breathe," breathing being the evidence of life in the Hebrew concept. Hence the Hebrew words for "living being" or "animal" (*chay*) and "life" (*chayyim*) derive from *chayah*. The verb is often used in Old Testament references suggesting that "living" is the result of doing the right thing (Deut. 4:1; 30:19, 20; Prov. 4:4; 9:6; Amos 5:4).[2]

Just, *tsaddiq.* One who is right, just, clear, clean, righteous; a person who is characterized by fairness, integrity, and justice in his dealings. . . . *Tsaddiq* is derived from the verb *tsadaq,* "to be righteous, justified, clear." *Tsaddiq* and its derivatives convey justice and integrity in one's life-style.[3]

Faith, *'emunah.* Firmness, stability, faithfulness, fidelity, conscientiousness, steadiness, certainty; that which is permanent, enduring, steadfast. *'Emunah* comes from the root *'aman,* "to be firm, sure, established, and steady." "Amen," derived from this same root, means, "it is firmly, truly so!" *'Emunah* is most often translated "faithfulness" or "truth," as this word denotes things that are unchanging and ultimately certain, as the truth is. This word appears in Habakkuk 2:4, "The just shall live by his *'emunah*," that is, his firmness, steadiness, and solid belief.[4]

THE BLESSINGS OF FAITHFULNESS

To be faithful is not just the performance of a duty, but it is a "full-of-faith" characteristic of our lives that brings blessings with it. There are the blessings of allowing the Lord to daily take our cares (Ps. 5:1–3), the blessings of seeing prayers answered (James 5:15, 16), and the blessings of living in wisdom (Matt. 7:24–27). Proverbs 28:20 says that the faithful man will "abound with blessings."

There are many blessings in store for the faithful, but faithfulness is something we are called to. Faithfulness requires that we do our part. This, in turn, releases—through *faith's action*—the operation of God's power, which brings faith's reward. In the following passages there is a picture of man's doing his part. No matter how small the part was, each person had something they did that was needed for God's will to be realized.

Write down all of the things that you see being done by God's faithful servants in each of these texts. What is "released" in each case of God's workings of power through faithful obedience?

Acts 12:5–10

      Man's action:

      God's action:

Acts 2:40–47

      Man's action:

      God's action:

Acts 8:26–38

      Man's action:

      God's action:

FAITH ALIVE

From your study what do you think is the most important thing about faithfulness in prayer? What makes this so important?

How would you describe the difference in the fruit of a faithful prayer life and a sporadic prayer life? Why do you think this is so?

Is your prayer life growing in faithfulness? Describe growth you may have seen in the recent past:

What factors have led to this growth pattern?

Take the time to review your answers and see what things are there that you would like to talk with the Lord about. You may have things you need help with, or you may want to praise Him for things you have seen Him doing.

FAITHFULNESS IN ACTION

In Joshua 10 there is a picture of faithfulness dramatized for us. Joshua and the troops of Israel were in battle with the armies of the Amorites. God had set Himself to do a mighty work on behalf of the children of Israel and, indeed, the battle was going their way. Joshua saw that the battle would not be complete before nightfall came, and a remnant of the enemy would escape.

It is at this point that Joshua stood, full of faith, and spoke the words recorded in Joshua 10:12, 13. He did the incredible, verbally commanding the sun and moon to stand still until final victory was won. In the sight of all Israel he made this request to the Lord, and God answered as he had prayed. This story is a marvelous picture of *intercession*, as the armies of Israel came to fight on behalf of an ally. It is also a great picture of *spiritual warfare,* as Joshua took dominion over the gods worshiped by the Amorites (sun and moon). But both became effective through Joshua's example of faithfulness.

Read the record of this event in Joshua 10:1–14 and use the questions below to help you study this picture of faithfulness.

Why is it that Israel fought for the Gibeonites? (See the background in Joshua 9.) How was Joshua leading Israel to be faithful in this way?

What was God's word to Israel regarding this battle? How did Israel's response show faith?

In light of God's word to Israel, how does Joshua's prayer for lengthening of the day show his faithfulness to complete what God called him to? How was this a response in faith to God's word?

FAITH ALIVE

After working through this lesson, how would you describe faithfulness? How would you explain its relationship with prayer? Can you see how fidelity to commitments and dependability to duty open the doorway to boldness in prayer's miraculous possibilities? Stop now and ask the Lord to work a greater faithfulness in you and to show you how you can develop this trait in your life.

1. *Spirit-Filled Life Bible* (Nashville, TN: Thomas Nelson Publishers, 1991), 1492, "Word Wealth: 11:22 faith."
2. Ibid., 1342, "Word Wealth: 2:4 shall live."
3. Ibid., 1145, "Word Wealth: 1:18 righteous."
4. Ibid., 920, "Word Wealth: 28:20 faithful."

Lesson 6/Intercession

How would you feel if the richest and most successful businessman in your line of work asked you to be his partner? You might wonder why he chose you, or you might muse over what you could possibly have to offer to the partnership. Mostly, you would probably feel honored at such a request and accept with little hesitation, especially if you were convinced of his genuine care and concern for you.

The fact is that God has asked us to partner with Him. As our Heavenly Father, He has asked you to join in the family business. His request is not based on anything you can do, but rather on who He has made you to be. He has made you to be His child and called you to be His ambassador on the earth. He places great value on your partnership because of His love for you.

It's sad to say, but many of God's children neglect the "business" that they have been asked to partner in. Most of the time this is because they simply don't understand the work they are to do. Wherever we turn, we may find Christians attempting almost every sort of righteous action—all sincere efforts at "helping" God, but too seldom actually "partnering with God." Partnership means to enter into *His* resources and to maximize by *His* power the release of the power He wants to work in and through us. "Helping God" is too often the unperceived opposite—seeking to get God to enter into *our* agenda or to bless *our* energetic efforts at our interpretation of His will. But there is a way to avoid the latter and gain discernment on the former—and prayer is the pathway to that discovery. Beginning prayer will bring us to the growing prayer privilege of intercession.

Intercessory prayer gets to the heart of our most powerful possibility as "partners with God." While intercession is certainly not the only thing that every one of us as believers are called to, it is definitely one of the foremost and primary assignments for our pursuit on which God expresses His heart. Let's take a two-step exercise: 1) Write out 1 Timothy 2:1, 2, capitalizing all the letters of the phrase "FIRST OF ALL." 2) Read through the scriptures listed below, using the following questions to help you learn about partnering with God through intercession. The "Word Wealth" section will guide you in this study.

What do you see God doing in this text?

What is He searching for?

What happens where there is no intercessor?

How is intercession partnering with the work that you see Jesus and the Holy Spirit doing?

How do they intercede for us?

 WORD WEALTH

Gap, *perets.* A break, gap, or breach; especially a gap in a wall. *Perets* comes from the verb *parats,* "to break forth, break open, or break down." Two verses (Is. 58:12; Amos 9:11) show that gaps or breaches need to be repaired; the former verse refers to the physical and spiritual ruins of Zion, and the latter to the tabernacle of David. In Ezekiel 22:30, "standing in the gap" is a metaphor for committed intercession. This refers to the gap between God and man that an intercessor tries to repair.[1]

Ezek. 22:30, 31

WORD WEALTH

Make intercession, *paga'*. To reach; to meet someone; to pressure or urge someone strongly; to meet up with a person; encounter, entreat; to assail with urgent petitions. In some passages *paga'* is translated "meet," as in Joshua 2:16. In Joshua 19:27 *paga'* refers to the extent to which a tribal boundary is reached. Sometimes the verb refers to "falling upon" someone in battle, that is, to meet up with the enemy with hostile intent (1 Kin. 2:29). *Paga'* is also translated "to make intercession," the idea being that a supplicant catches up with a superior, and reaches him with an urgent request. Thus, intercession involves reaching God, meeting God, and entreating Him for His favor.[2]

Is. 53:12

WORD WEALTH

Make intercession, *entunchano*. To fall in with, meet with in order to converse. From this description of a casual encounter, the word progresses to the idea of pleading with a person on behalf of another, although at times the petition may be against another (Acts 25:24; Rom. 11:2).[3]

Rom. 8:26–28

Heb. 7:24, 25

1 John 2:1

FAITH ALIVE

Can you clearly describe the difference between "helping" God and "partnering" with Him? Write your thoughts or your feelings about the idea of being a direct partner in what the Lord is doing. How can you best go about that?

How important to you is it to see mercy and deliverance (salvation) come where judgment is due? What can you do to make this happen?

Define "intercession" as you are coming to understand it, and relate its importance to spiritual endeavor.

How would you reshape your prayer life to indicate intercession's importance?

JOINING GOD'S WILL WITH MAN'S WANT

Psalm 23 begins by stating that since the Lord is my Shepherd, I have no want. There is nothing lacking of my needs, because the Good Shepherd meets them all. This is God's plan for all of humankind: to meet our needs.

However, once we have learned the pathway of following our Great Shepherd and learned the blessing of having Him meet our needs, He invites us to learn the way of prayer that begins to carry the needs of others before His throne. There are hosts of lost or straying sheep for whom our prayers "stand in the gap." It is a phenomenal fact that the Almighty God has invited us to be the prayer instruments by which these lost sheep begin to find the Shepherd's heart and provision for them.

Because it is God's desire to meet every person's needs, He calls us to intercede—to place ourselves between the needs of others and the will of God in order to bring them together. Of course, God is fully able to take action toward others by His own sovereign will and power—bypassing our role in prayer completely. But the amazing fact is that He hasn't and He doesn't. Instead, His sovereign choice is to act only in response to the prayers of His people. He not only *invites* our partnership; He *insists* upon it.

Read through these next scriptures to see examples of intercession. Write down a definition of intercession that is unique to each scripture.

1 Sam. 14:45

2 Sam. 23:11, 12

Ezek. 22:30

1 John 2:1, 2

What things are alike in each of these scriptures?

What things are different?

By combining the above definitions into a comprehensive statement, write your complete definition of intercession:

FAITH ALIVE

How does your definition of intercession fit into your prayer life? Think through and write the difference between your devotional time with Christ on a daily basis, and your times of intercession for others. What are the characteristics of each aspect of prayer—devotion compared with intercession?

What things do you think you may need to learn to apply in order for you to grow into intercession as you would like to?

Take the time to pray over these things before you continue this study. Then, find someone to partner with you in prayer who will help you to be accountable to see these things developed in your life.

LIVING EXAMPLES OF INTERCESSION

Throughout the Old Testament intercession is seen as a part of God's plan for His people, and it is exhibited in the lives of some of Scripture's most well-known personalities. With these godly men as role models, let's pursue learning more about this powerful part of God's plan for our prayer potential.

There is no better way to learn than by example. Once we can see something in action, some of the mystery is removed, and understanding comes more easily. With this in mind, read through the scriptures listed below and use the study questions to help direct your thoughts. Each of these examples of intercession gives important insight into the practical working of this type of prayer.

EXAMPLE 1: <u>Abraham intercedes for Sodom and Gomorrah—Gen. 18:17–33</u>

What does the Lord indicate is motivating His choosing to tell His plans to Abraham? What are these plans? (vv. 17–19)

What question does Abraham ask the Lord in response? (v. 23)

What are Abraham's concerns? How are these consistent with God's character? (vv. 24, 25)

What do you note about Abraham's listening to the Lord's response during this time of intercession? What is God's response to Abraham's intercession? (vv. 26–33)

EXAMPLE 2: <u>Moses intercedes for Israel—Ex. 32:31–35; 33:7–14</u>

What was the crisis setting of this intercessory meeting? (32:1–31)

What is Moses' prayer?

What do we learn about the nature of Moses' walk with the Lord? (33:9–11)

What is the first focus of Moses' intercession and what does God say? (vv. 12–14)

What reasons does Moses give for desiring God to spare Israel? (vv. 15, 16a)

How do these reasons relate to God's character? How do they relate to God's honor? (vv. 16b, 17)

Note the privilege God allowed Moses to realize as a result of His unselfish intercession (vv. 18–23). What might we expect of our own relationship with God if we set ourselves for intercession like this?

LIVING EXAMPLES CONTINUED

In Abraham and Moses we see intercessors who were praying directly for others while their own situations were secure (that is, they were not personally experiencing the crisis;

or, as in these examples, God's judgment). While this is often the case when we intercede, there are times when we will be more directly involved with the needs that we are praying about, as in the following examples from the Bible.

Read through these scriptures and see what insight you gain from these stories of men who interceded for a situation they were personally involved in.

EXAMPLE 3: <u>David intercedes for his son: 2 Sam. 12:13–23</u>

What does David do as he prays? What is he seeking?

What is God's answer to David's prayer? How does David respond to this?

How does David's refusal to live in defeat show a pure faith in God?

EXAMPLE 4: <u>Daniel intercedes for Israel: Dan. 9:1–19</u>

What leads Daniel to pray? How is his stance in prayer based in God's Word? (vv. 1–4)

What physical things does Daniel do as he prays? (v. 3) What kind of heart toward the Lord does this show? (v. 4a)

List the ways in which Daniel fully identifies himself with the sins and needs of Israel. Does he separate himself from them in his prayer? (vv. 5–11)

What does he say about the Lord's justice? What does Israel deserve? (vv. 12–14) What is he asking for? (vv. 15–19)

Even though Daniel has walked righteously, he still—in intercession— identifies with the sinfulness of those for whom he prays. What might you learn to apply in prayer as you study both Moses' and Daniel's unself-righteous stance in prayer?

EXAMPLE 5: Jesus, the Perfect Example

As always, Jesus is the ultimate example, and in the case of intercession, He is a study of the True Intercessor. Remember that the *words* of a prayer are not all that an intercessor says, for the *actions* of his life will speak volumes. Jesus not only prayed for us as He prayed for all believers (John 17) and now continues to intercede for us at the right hand of God the Father (Heb. 7:25; 8:1), but He became the Perfect Intercessor in that He placed His life in the gap for you and me (Is. 53:12; 59:16, 17). This is the ultimate picture of intercession. Take three steps:

1. Note the Isaiah passages. Do you see Jesus described as an Intercessor? Reflect on Isaiah 53 and note the things Jesus did (a) that fulfilled this prophecy; (b) as an intercessory *action*.

2. The night before Jesus died, He prayed a great, timeless prayer of intercession—John 17. (a) List the key things for which He prays; (b) How many times does He pray for unity ("that they may be one")?

3. According to Hebrews 7:25 and 8:1, where is Jesus right now, and what is He doing—and why? What might we learn from this as to (a) reasons for our being restfully confident; and (b) actions that model how our prayer life should be activated?

 FAITH ALIVE

What points of intercession have you seen that you can apply now? Write ways you hope to put these into action.

Make a prayer list for your times of intercession. Include the names of people, nations, churches, ministries, social and moral issues, and so on. You may want to refer to chapter 3 and review the first section about what we are to pray for.

1. *Spirit-Filled Life Bible* (Nashville, TN: Thomas Nelson Publishers, 1991), 1186, "Word Wealth: 22:30 gap."

2. Ibid., 1097–98, "Word Wealth: 27:18 make intercession."

3. Ibid., 1880, "Word Wealth: 7:25 make intercession."

Lesson 7/Spiritual Warfare

No bombs fell, no guns were fired, no one was killed, yet there was great violence. The earth was shaken, prison doors were opened, guards were overcome, and indeed, warfare took place. But this was not the warfare of man against man in physical battle, though physical results occurred. This was spiritual warfare that was initiated in prayer.

It began as two missionaries were preaching the gospel and came into direct confrontation with a demonized woman. They proceeded to command the spirit to release her in Jesus' name, and the demon left her. But as in most battles, there are few immediately decisive victories. There came satanic counterattack as people were stirred up by this incident and the missionaries thrown into jail.

From there the battle raged on as these two men set themselves to warfare through prayers and praise to God. In a short time the chains that bound them and doors that held them in were unlocked by a mighty earthquake. This answer to prayer was not the end of this battle. The opportunity was then at hand to speak the gospel to the keeper of the prison, and his whole household received salvation that night.

This powerful example of a spiritual battle is recorded in Acts 16:16–34. Stop now, and read through this entire passage. Review the above after you've read it; see how each phrase applies. Now, use this text to answer the questions below:

What kinds of freedom were received by (a) the servant girl, (b) Paul and Silas, and (c) the jailer through spiritual warfare?

How did this battle open the doors for each of the individuals?

Can you see how Paul's and Silas's incarceration may be a retaliation of the evil spirit they cast out, as surely as a retaliatory attitude of evil businessmen? What lesson may be learned in this light?

What response did Paul and Silas have to the situation? What tools did they use in warfare?

 FAITH ALIVE

How do Bible stories like this affect you? Do you find yourself thinking of the circumstance as something for another time and place? Think about this for a moment.

It is often easy to look at the great miracles that God has done and think that they will never happen here and now. It's not that we don't believe God can do these things today, or even that we think He won't. It simply seems that we have difficulty imagining them happening and our having a key role in the situation.

What are some situations in which you would like to see God do mighty and transforming things? Be realistic with your heart's cry for a visitation of God's grace. Don't hesitate to at least write out the "vision" for prayer He may put in your heart.

THE NATURE OF OUR WARFARE

The war is ceaseless—going on all around us all the time, even though we may not see it or even be aware of its presence. Have you ever read passages of Scripture as just now, and still wondered what spiritual warfare really is? In many parts of the Bible we see examples of it, but because the text doesn't use the words, "This is spiritual warfare," many do not understand what is taking place in the invisible realm.

To understand spiritual warfare, first let's think about what war is. Simply stated, war is the conflict that occurs when one party seeks to gain by force something that another party will not willingly concede, or when both parties desire to possess a thing that cannot be mutually shared.

Spiritual warfare is the battle that continues between the armies of God and the forces of the Devil. It is not poetry or play; it is real, and its plunder is the souls of free-willed human beings. If it were merely a matter of power, the Almighty God could master the Prince of Darkness in a moment. But because the ebb and flow of battle depends upon the will of humans—to receive or reject divine rule; to believe or refuse divine grace—the struggle for minds and bodies goes on. The Adversary, who hates everything that even remotely bears God's image, hates and seeks to control man.

The following scriptures teach us how to be effective soldiers in God's army. As you read them, use the questions to help you gain a greater understanding of the nature of this warfare.

Luke 11:2: According to Jesus' words, the objective of your warfare is the dominion of one power's will over another. Define this on the basis of the text.

Matt. 16:18, 19: How does Jesus describe the objective in both positive and negative terms? ("Gates" refers to the ancient seat of military councils.)

Luke 12:31; Col. 1:13: Describe the two kingdoms engaged in battle.

Matt. 6:13: What common prayer expresses our assurance of victory? Illustrations of this: examine Peter (Luke 22:31) and Paul (2 Cor. 12:7–9) and describe the situations wherein they were "delivered" unto victory.

EQUIPPING FOR BATTLE

The reality of the spiritual struggle calls us each to learn the wisdom of appropriate preparation. The passage indicated below is the classic and complete directive for equipping for battle in the spiritual war—the battle in "the heavenlies"; that is, "the invisible realm of spiritual conflict" that surrounds us all—always.

Eph. 6:10–18

What are your directives as you approach the battle? (vv. 10, 11)

What is the nature of your opponent, and what description do we have of his troops? (v. 12)

Why are you to wear God's armor, and what promise is contained in this directive? (v. 13)

What is to be your constant stance in battle? How might this be done? Use your own words. (v. 14a)

How is the armor dependent upon your living in God's provision rather than your own works? (v. 14b)

 AT A GLANCE

Let's take a thorough look at "the armor of God." Following are six of the key words descriptive of the spiritual significance of this armor to be used in an invisible, but deadly real battle. First, read through the descriptions and the "Word Wealth" section that follow. Then, take the key idea of each piece and translate it into its behavioral application; that is, if you are going to put this armor on, how will it affect your living and your praying? Use the space marked "Behavioral Application" following each piece of equipment discussed and describe your anticipated response to this text as you equip for battle.

THE ARMOR OF GOD'S ARMY

EQUIPMENT	TEXT	NOTES ON USAGE
WHOLE ARMOR	Eph. 6:13	This armor is prepared that you may withstand every onslaught of the Adversary. Be sure to make use of the full armor, for taking only selected portions will leave you vulnerable to attack (Luke 12:1–5). Jesus warns us of such foolishness and hypocrisy, saying it will lead to disaster (Matt. 7:26, 27).

TRUTH	Eph. 6:14	Truth is what holds the armor in place. Without having a firm grasp on the truth, your armor will have gaps that present an unprotected target for the foe to attack. Carefully study the Word of Truth (2 Tim. 2:15) and heed the sound teaching of godly leaders (Acts 2:42) in order to be filled with the truth and therefore prepared for battle.

Behavioral Application:

RIGHTEOUSNESS	Eph. 6:14	"Living in righteousness" is the breastplate—the body armor that protects your most vital parts. This is also referred to as the breastplate of faith and love (1 Thess. 5:8), signifying that in the kingdom of God, the fulfillment of all law (and therefore right standing) is love (Matt. 22:37–40); and entry into the kingdom is only by faith unto righteousness (Rom. 10:4–10).

Behavioral Application:

GOSPEL OF PEACE	Eph. 6:15	The gospel of peace—the message of salvation through Jesus Christ, which brings peace with God (Rom. 5:1–5)— is the warrior's shoes. "How beautiful are the <u>feet</u> of those who preach the gospel of peace . . ." (Rom. 10:15). Nothing can give your feet a firmer stance than to be

fully dependent upon the un-
shakable and unchangeable
ground of the gospel (Rev. 14:6).

Behavioral Application:

FAITH   Eph. 6:16   The constant attack of the
                                   enemy will seek to discourage
                                   and demoralize you. But the
                                   shield of faith will provide pro-
                                   tection against these attacks,
                                   "quenching," that is, *swallowing
                                   up* the enemy's firepower. Re-
                                   member never to base your
                                   faith upon your own strengths,
                                   which is folly, but your faith-
                                   shield must be placed in God
                                   and His power to overcome the
                                   enemy (Prov. 3:5–8).

Behavioral Application:

SALVATION   Eph. 6:17   Salvation is the helmet that pro-
                                   tects your head. This shows us
                                   that God's salvation is not only
                                   the acceptance of Jesus' death
                                   and resurrection unto forgive-
                                   ness, but refers also to the com-
                                   plete redemptive process, which
                                   includes the renewing of our
                                   minds (Rom. 12:1, 2). This is
                                   found in a living commitment to
                                   walking with the Lord daily.

Behavioral Application:

WORD OF GOD   Eph. 6:17   Your primary weapon is the sharpest of blades, which cannot be dulled by time and usage (Heb. 4:12). The wielding of this powerful sword not only defeats the foe but strengthens and directs the warrior as well (Ps. 119:105). This weapon is to be sheathed within our own hearts in order to prevent us from becoming a captive of the enemy (Ps. 119:11).

Behavioral Application:

    ## WORD WEALTH

(To be examined before beginning the "Behavioral Application" of each armor piece. Lay hold of the richness of meaning in each word as it bears on the "arming" of oneself.)

Gospel, *euangelion.* Compare "evangel," "evangelize," "evangelistic." In ancient Greece *euangelion* designated the reward given for bringing good news. Later it came to mean the good news itself. In the New Testament the word includes both the promise of salvation and its fulfillment by the life, death, resurrection, and ascension of Jesus Christ. *Euangelion* also designates the written narratives of Matthew, Mark, Luke, and John.[1]

Faith, *pistis.* Conviction, confidence, trust, belief, reliance, trustworthiness, and persuasion. In the New Testament setting, *pistis* is the divinely implanted principle of inward confidence, assurance, trust, and reliance in God and all that He says. The word sometimes denotes the object or the content of belief (Acts 6:7; 14:22; Gal. 1:23).[2]

Peace, *eirene.* A state of rest, quietness, and calmness; an absence of strife; tranquility. It generally denotes a perfect well-being. *Eirene* includes harmonious relationships between God and men, men and men, nations, and families. Jesus as

Prince of Peace gives peace to those who [live under His lordship.][3]

Righteousness, *diakaiosune.* Just, the quality of being right. Broadly, the word suggests conformity to the revealed will of God in all respects. *Diakaiosune* is both judicial and gracious. God declares the believer righteous, in the sense of acquitting him, and imparts righteousness to him (2 Cor. 5:21).[4]

Truth, *alethuo.* Derived from negative, *a,* and *lanthano,* "to be hidden," "to escape notice." *Alethia* is the opposite of fictitious, feigned or false. It denotes veracity, reality, sincerity, accuracy, integrity, truthfulness, dependability, and propriety in the spoken word.[5] This word is used most notably of doctrine or teaching.

Salvation, *soterion.* Rescue, deliverance, safety, liberation, release, preservation, and the general word for Christian salvation. This form is only used five times in the New Testament. In most places *soteria,* the generic form, is used. It is an all-inclusive word signifying forgiveness, healing, prosperity, deliverance, safety, rescue, liberation, and restoration. This bespeaks the fact that Christ's salvation is total in scope, covering every part of man and his life.[6]

 FAITH ALIVE

Seeing the armor that God provides, what assurance do you feel as you head toward battle?

What new things have you learned about this armor that will help you use it more effectively?

Which part of the armor most stands out to you? What, in your opinion, sets this apart from the others?

What portions of God's armor do you feel most secure in the use of? Which do you feel least confident about? Why do you think this is so?

JOINING THE BATTLE

How often have we all seen old war movies where a young soldier, just finished with training, enthusiastically looks forward to actual combat. No true soldier ever enjoyed waiting, because it puts the battle's timing into the hands of the enemy. To take the offensive stance provides certain elements of control.

We understand, of course, that the issues in this spiritual war are not under our control, but the Lord's. However, after some basic training, we may feel like those enthusiastic soldiers who can hardly wait to join the spiritual battle. This desire is not borne from the heart of someone looking for an opportunity to destroy others, but the stance of one who knows he or she can actually do something to change the eternal outcome of the battle for human souls. Through prayer's power (Eph. 6:18), when equipped with spiritual resources (2 Cor. 10:3–5; Eph. 6:12–17), we have been given all the firepower that we will ever need. We've also been given the guarantee of ultimate victory (Matt. 16:18), verified by Christ's resurrection from the dead (Rev. 1:18).

With this assurance—God is "for us," on our side (Rom. 8:31)—we are ready to look forward to warfare; but how do we begin? The war is in constant motion all around us; how do we join in? Study the scriptures below to find the answer.

What does Ephesians 6:18 say to do?

How does Jesus show you in Luke 11:2 to seek God's kingdom?

What is the incense offered that ushers in the establishment of God's kingdom with power? (Rev. 5:8; 8:3, 4)

After looking at these scriptures, what would you define as being the first step of joining into battle? (Remember 1 Tim. 2:1–8.)

We have discovered that prayer is the action of attack, the joining of the battle. What are to be the boundaries of our prayers? Case study: Paul's prayer for the Ephesians' expansive readying of soul (3:14–21) as they prepare for battle (6:10–18).

 ### FAITH ALIVE

Now that you have completed this introduction to spiritual warfare, take some time to record your thoughts.

What are the primary things on your mind about this warfare?

Is it a new thing for you to think of yourself as a soldier? How does it make you feel?

Do you find yourself to be an eager or reluctant soldier? What would you do to make yourself more confident and anticipatory of joining the fight?

Are there any areas in your life that you believe will not be involved in this warfare? Why?

Are there any questions that this study has brought to your mind? Write them down so that you can come back to them as you find answers for them further in the study.

To conclude: Write out these verses to secure confidence that if you enter His service, you *will* win!

Rom. 8:37–39

2 Cor. 2:14

1 John 4:4

1. *Spirit-Filled Life Bible* (Nashville, TN: Thomas Nelson Publishers, 1991), 1468, "Word Wealth: 1:1 gospel."
2. Ibid., "Word Wealth: 11:22 faith."
3. Ibid., 1510, "Word Wealth: 1:79 peace."
4. Ibid., 1857, "Word Wealth: 4:8 righteousness."
5. Ibid., 774, "Word Wealth: 5:5 truth."
6. Ibid., 1682, "Word Wealth: 28:28 salvation."

Lesson 8/The Unseen War

Surprise attack: The ability to strike on the enemy's position when he is unprepared for or unaware of your presence. This strategy has long been effective in war—was the means that instigated America's response and entry into World War II—and, for good or ill, is considered a strategic advantage in battle.

The development of stealth technology, costing governments billions of dollars and years of work, is but the latest in this quest for secrecy and surprise in attempting to gain military superiority. Yet, as much as we know and observe such enterprise in the physical/political realm, how few realize that in the midst of their day-to-day life, a constant barrage of invisible weapons is being levelled in an unseen world. These weapons may not be discussed over the bargaining table of international diplomacy, but they are wreaking havoc amid a public that is blind to the nature of this war.

Many believe that this war is as silent as its weapons are invisible, but daily there are explosions heard that shake our world: Aids! Cancer! Divorce! Violence! So the bombs hit, devastating individuals, families, and society with this nonstop holocaust.

Far worse than any sci-fi attack of aliens bent on destruction of this earth, we endure the attack of an enemy that seeks to enslave and kill our entire population. Not H. G. Wells's *War of the Worlds,* but a real, yet invisible, war is being fought over this planet.

This can begin to sound quite tragic, but remember this hope: We have weapons that can repel this invasion! The spiritual artillery that we possess can unleash more power than any weapon ever conceived by man. And yet, even though God has equipped us with great resources for battle, we must remember that we will not be successful if we are a divided army. We must unify our resistance in order to win the battle.

This lesson is designed to help you answer questions about the enemy, and to better understand our battlefield—the spiritual realm. In military terms, this is an "intelligence mission." It is always a strategic advantage in warfare to know your enemy—both his strengths and weaknesses—and to be familiar with the terrain where the battles will be fought.

Use the following questions to help you establish biblical facts about the spiritual world, as they apply to each of the scriptures listed below.

How do statements of Jesus and others in the Bible verify the reality of this realm? How can we become aware of actions in the spiritual realm? What is the scope of its impact? How can you personally impact what happens in the invisible?

2 Kin. 6:15–17

Dan. 10:1–21

Luke 11:14–26

John 1:1–5, 14–18

Eph. 6:12

1 John 4:1–6

 ## BEHIND THE SCENES

In New Testament times the word *demon* meant "evil spirit." The Bible teaches that a personal devil [Satan] is assisted by evil spirits in opposition to the work of God, and contrary to the welfare of people (Mark 3:22–26; Rev. 12:9). Some biblical examples of demonic attacks are: afflicting people with evil purposes (1 Tim. 4:1, 2); mental derangement (Matt. 8:28, 29); and physical illness (Mark 9:17–27). It is important to clarify at this point that not all such illnesses and afflictions are the result of demonic influence.

The climates of the physical and spiritual realms can and do impact each other. If this were not true, then God would not be concerned with the physical actions of people, which He is; and demons could not cause any physical malady, which scripture shows they can (Mark 9:17–27). Yet, though the impact of sin present in our race has introduced disease and illness of body, mind, and spirit, every single occurrence of such sickness cannot be traced to a direct sin or bondage (Rom. 5:12).

It has been incorrectly assumed by some that mental illness or certain mental conditions are always attributable to demonic attack. However, we should never assume that a physical or mental condition is the direct result of a person's sins or spiritual oppression. Our place is to listen sensitively to the Holy Spirit's direction as we seek to appropriately minister Jesus' life to hurting individuals.

Evil spirits only have access to the human personality (that is, demonic bondage) through an element of sinful consent, if not deliberate choice or succession of choices, by individuals who will be held responsible for their actions. The idea that evil spirits can arbitrarily control or oppress people at their own will is inconsistent with scripture in that it takes from people the responsibility for their sins. Demonic bondage occurs when people make a choice to submit ongoingly to the will of the demon luring or leading them into sin. This is not usually the result of a single instance of failure in a Christian's walk, but It is the foul fruit of a person's walking in that sin—pursuing it in the flesh—for a season of time.

The reality of demonic bondage has often been misunderstood to the point of evoking fear in some people. Some have misinterpreted the account of the seven sons of Sceva (Acts 19:1–16) and are afraid that they are not spiritually mature enough to wage warfare against demonic forces. But the error of the sons of Sceva was twofold: 1) they assumed that they could exorcise demons by a set formula; and 2) they tried to function in Jesus' name, having no authority to do so as they were not believers. However, you and I can thereby learn to function in contrast to their failure. Functioning in the power of Jesus' name requires personal submission to His lordship. Further, we ought never to rely upon set formulas to establish God's work, for it is always His *power,* His *presence,* and His *timing* that fulfill His plan. Jesus said pointedly that those who believe in Him would cast out demons in His name (Mark 16:17). Further, Ephesians 6:10–18 reminds us that spiritual warfare in prayer is the responsibility of every believer. We need to find our place in this ministry.

Sadly, there are many people in our world today who are afflicted by spiritual bondage. Jesus sends us to minister His love and power to them. And as we do, we can be confident, because there is no power of evil greater than the power of God. Christ has full authority over all Satan's evil purposes, demonically begotten physical maladies, and hellishly fomented minds. He wants to use you and me to offer help to all in those extremities.[1]

 KINGDOM EXTRA

In Luke 11:24 Jesus says that an exorcised spirit goes to seek rest in the "dry" places. In light of Jesus' words that He gives water that causes rivers of living water to spring up "into everlasting life" (John 4:13, 14), "dry places" could be defined as "areas where the living water has not reached."

Using a concordance or topical Bible, look up other New Testament references that speak of life in the spiritual realm. Below is a list of words or themes that you may want to include in this study. As you read through what each scripture has to say, write down the things that you observe. Let this serve as an outline to help weave together all that you learn about the invisible from further study and experience. (This is a prompter toward extended examination. Use separate pieces of paper—perhaps for each word or phrase—and write your observations about key texts you discover.)

angel	kingdom of heaven,	adversary
unclean spirit	kingdom of God	enemy
heavenlies	heavenly host	spirit(s)
the blood of Jesus	principalities and powers	
Devil, Satan	demon(s)	

This list may prompt discoveries that make you want to add to it. Do so as you continue your study.

 ## FAITH ALIVE

Though the Scriptures clearly teach there is an invisible realm of spiritual action all around us, some succumb to notions that biblical references to the spiritual realm are only figurative.

However, this view requires a belief that Jesus would have allowed people to go on believing in things that were not real, or that He would have simply allowed people to continue with false superstitions, which is not consistent with His character nor His teachings.

Why do you think some would choose to deny the spiritual realm when Scripture is so clear on the subject?

It is sometimes easy to become intimidated by people who don't believe in the spiritual realm and be hesitant to openly share our viewpoint for fear of others' ridiculing us as "believers in fairy tales." How can we sensitively, yet honestly, respond to their questions?

THE NATURE OF SPIRITUAL POWERS

In 1969 the whole world watched as, for the first time, man set foot on the moon. This "giant leap for mankind" let us see firsthand just what another world might be like.

We watched men bounce around without the same tug of gravity we experience on earth, holding—limiting movement. We witnessed the suits that they wore to provide oxygen and a stable and livable environment. The view was of a dead world, drastically different from the life that abounds here on earth.

Years were spent in study and preparation before man ever reached the moon. It is obvious by the suits that were worn that research had been directed toward knowing in advance what the moon would be like as a living environment. Care had to be taken to insure that the astronauts could survive.

When you face the reality of dealing with another "world" or realm, there are questions to be asked: What features of this world are like your own? What features are different? What are the essential laws that control this world?

These same questions need to be asked as you prepare to function in the spiritual world. In the verses below there are many facts to learn about the invisible realm. Some things are just like our physical world, and some are very different.

What are the four defined levels of demonic authority listed in Ephesians 6:12?

Compare this to Revelation 12:7 where Michael is shown to have angels under his charge. How does this show a structure of authority in the spiritual realm?

Read Matthew 12:25–30. Why is it so important that believers remain united in warfare?

Why do demonic forces work together?

What does Jesus say of those who are not with Him?

Read Luke 10:1–10. What do these parables show about the dynamic potential of the kingdom of God? Outline the assignment Jesus gave the seventy. What mention of demons is there?

Read Luke 10:17–24. What had the disciples discovered, having gone on their assignment?

What was their feeling about this?

What was Jesus' response?

Note Luke 10:21. See how Jesus *both* approves and cautions regarding this realm of supernatural ministry. What do you feel we might learn that will balance both boldness-unto-action with sensitive-humility-and-wisdom?

   FAITH ALIVE

Trying to relate to something unseen can be a difficult thing. Many people have trouble understanding or dealing with the reality of the invisible world.

What difficulties have you experienced in relating to the spiritual realm in the past?

What has been the hardest issue for you to relate to?

Has this study section helped you recognize the authority structures in the spiritual realm? Write a declaration of your confidence in Christ as you accept your place in the spiritual battle. Perhaps you might start with reading the following texts: Romans 8:37–39; 2 Corinthians 10:3–5; Colossians 2:14; 1 John 4:4; Revelation 12:10.

What do you expect to see happen in your prayer life as you comprehend more of the spiritual realm?

THE UNCEASING FIGHT

We may be amazed to learn that during the World War I there was actually a break in fighting for the celebration of Christmas. It has been recorded that in some places opposing troops even shared the joyous occasion together, yet tragically returned to their own battlements the next day to fire on those with whom they had laughed and sung the night before.

We may suppose there are breaks in the spiritual conflict, but the Adversary is relentless. What does 1 Peter 5:6–9 tell us in this regard?

The war that rages in the spiritual realm is not one that experiences moments of rest or reprieve. Read the verses listed here and record what they say about this ongoing battle and how we should respond to it. Use these questions to help you focus on this subject: How are you to stand in warfare? What is your mind-set to be toward the battle? What are you to pursue in your life as a soldier? What things should not be motivating factors? Where is your power found? (Note the following word studies related to these texts.)

Ps. 35:1–3

Phil. 1:27–30

1 Tim. 6:6–12

2 Tim. 2:3–5

 WORD WEALTH

Sober, *nepho.* To be sober, having not consumed any intoxicating agent; to be watchful, discreet. The key for us in spiritual warfare is that we do not allow ourselves to become intoxicated by the things that we will see, but rather keep our focus on what Christ has done for us (Luke 10:17–20).

Steadfast, *stereos.* Solid, stable, steadfast, strong, sure. This word teaches us that our stance is not only to be firm and unmovable but complete, relating to every area of our life.

Vigilant, *gregoreuo.* To watch, to refrain from sleep. This is derived from the word, *egeiro,* "to rouse." In the New Testament *gregoreuo* is used in a spiritual as well as physical sense. This is the word Jesus used when He said, "Could you not <u>watch</u> one hour?" and "<u>Watch</u> and pray, lest you enter into temptation" (Matt. 26:40, 41).

FAITH ALIVE

Review this lesson. As you put your thoughts in order, reflect upon the things that you have learned. Make a list of those things that have been new or deepened insights for you.

Do you think that knowing these things might have changed any key responses you have made or actions taken before now? How? How do you anticipate these discoveries affecting you in the future?

What spiritual responses will you need, what decisions will you make, to apply these new insights?

The key to Christian growth is living in what the Lord has taught you. Write down a prayer asking the Lord to help you live in the new truths that He has taught you about spiritual warfare.

---

1. Based on *The Wesley Bible* (Nashville, TN: Thomas Nelson Publishers, 1990), 1523, "Focus Note: Demon Possession (Luke 4:33–36)."

Lesson 9/Going into Battle

At the beginning of the Civil War the general mind-set in the North was anything but realistic. It is well recorded that crowds of civilians followed the troops to the first great battle, carrying picnic lunches and prepared for an outing much as we would prepare for a football or baseball game. They hoped that they would be provided with an enjoyable performance before they packed up their baskets and returned home.

The thought of real warfare was not in their minds, and few had any idea of the pain and suffering that would follow in the years to come. The reality of lost lives and maimed soldiers had not yet begun, and the misguided notion of most was that the Southerners would simply pack up and go home as soon as guns were fired.

It was a warm day as the Northern soldiers marched toward their first confrontation, and many of them began to lay aside their gear because it was too cumbersome on such a hot day. Soldiers arrived at the front without ammunition and other supplies needed for battle. Many walked at their own pace rather than trying to stay with their companies.

During that first battle, the North was badly defeated because they had not prepared for a real battle. There was little thought given to actual training or troop discipline, and the strategy was merely to "just show up and win the battle."

It's more illustrative than we care to acknowledge—that this is the way many Christians think of spiritual warfare. They neglect appropriate training; they aren't prepared with the proper armaments; and they don't understand, or won't accept, the concept of the spiritual authority intended to be exercised by their commanding officers (that is, their pastors and leaders). How are Christians supposed to prepare for warfare? Psalm 5 presents a vivid picture of preparing in prayer for battle. Study this next section to learn how God intends to have you prepared for the battles you will face.

In Psalm 5:2, 3, how does the psalmist begin his days?

In verses 4–6, as he directs his prayers to the Lord, note his grounds for pleading against the enemy he faces.

Analyze verses 7–12. Recognizing that this song is a prayerful address to the Lord in the face of an opponent, note the ways.

(a) the warrior prays for protection and help.
(b) the enemy's character and tactics are discerned.
(c) the specific way defeat of the enemy is requested.

Now, apply these ideas to a situation you are aware of in the present scene of our society.

 WORD WEALTH

Direct, *'arak.* To arrange, put in order (in a very wide variety of applications). To put or set (oneself or the battle) in array; order, compare, direct, equal, esteem, estimate, expert (in war), furnish, handle, join (in warfare), ordain, prepare. The wide range of possible translations for this word is particularly significant to this lesson as it points out the many areas needed in preparation for spiritual warfare.

This Hebrew word *'arak,* "direct," is used in the following scripture passages relating to warfare. Next to each text is written the English word or words used to translate the meaning of *'arak.* Using these Old Testament settings in which the

battles waged between the people of the Lord and the enemies of His people, let us draw lessons in principle. Note what
truths you find as you see this word used in other contexts.
Relate these to what your prayer is to accomplish in the spiritual realm each day. (The phrase after the text is the way
'arak is translated in that verse.)

Lev. 6:12 (and lay . . . in order)

Lev. 27:8 (shall set a value for him)

Judg. 20:22 (formed the battle line)

1 Sam. 17:8 (to line up for battle)

2 Sam. 10:9, 10 (put them in battle array)

1 Chr. 12:33 (expert in war)

Jer. 46:3 (order)

WORD WEALTH

Watchman, *tsaphah.* To look out, to peer into the distance, to watch, keep watch, wait for, observe, spy, look up, look well; to scope out, especially in order to see approaching danger, and to warn those who are endangered. This verb occurs eighty times and is often translated "watchmen," referring to the king's guards (1 Sam. 14:16) or those who look out from the city wall (2 Kin. 9:17, 18). In other instances it is spiritual watchmen, or prophets, who look out, see danger, and report to the people (Is. 52:8; Jer. 6:17).[1] In this lesson it shows expectancy toward, watching and waiting for the Lord's answer to prayer, along with the picture of a lookout or scout gaining information needed for battle strategy.

"Watching" in prayer may be fulfilled by attentiveness to events taking place in the society around you, and rather than merely "talking about" political or international or socially troubling events, *praying* with faith and power. "Watching" in prayer is also fulfilled by waiting upon the Lord and allowing the Holy Spirit to speak to your heart—to give direction and discernment regarding individuals or difficult circumstances.

FAITH ALIVE

In the light of the word studies just pursued, set your heart to consider the following with openness.

1. Take a moment to assess the preparation factors in your own life-style. How do you spiritually prepare yourself for each day's events?

2. How do you pray about upcoming events in your life?

3. Take a moment to contemplate the content of your prayers. Are your prayers usually specific or general? Do they lean toward emotionless, ritualistic duty, or heartfelt compassion and yearning? Do you find yourself often preoccupied with personal requests, praying personal preferences, or are you truly seeking to discern God's will in each matter as you pray?

4. Do you have a plan or strategy for your prayer times, or do you approach prayer spontaneously, without much forethought?

5. How would you go about preparing for a time of focused, intercessory prayer?

HONOR WORTH FIGHTING FOR

In the Middle Ages knights would joust over the issue of honor. During colonial times the duel was with swords or pistols; later, a shoot-out on some dusty Western street would settle the score, but the reasons were the same. To some, even the smallest backward glance was reason to kill, while others killed only as an act of self-defense or to protect their loved ones from danger.

Whether in a courtroom clash, a Western brawl, or a modern-day, drive-by shooting, people still fight to defend their honor, however misguided their motives. The violation of honor can be petty or great, depending on the pride of the individual. Nonetheless, history records many fights, feuds, battles, and wars that hinged on someone's pride.

As believers in Jesus Christ, such personal judgments should be left behind. That is not to say that we are called to let the world "roll over us." On the contrary, we are called to overcome the world, not by physical force, but through spiritual warfare.

In spiritual battle we are soldiers who seek to bring honor to our King, Jesus. The charge of every believer is to bring glory to God (Matt. 5:16), and it is this honor—God's, not ours—that is worth fighting for.

The Bible records many stories about those who fought to defend God's honor—with physical action as well as spiritual. As you read these passages, outline the words and actions of the persons involved, then their prayers, and then the results of their warfare. In each episode, write what you can see of the individual's "heart" for God and relationship with Him. At the end, note a lesson in prayer warfare and *its motive* as you may apply it to yourself.

1 Sam. 17:1–11, 20–24, 32–52

(a) Words/Action

(b) Prayer

(c) Results

(d) The "heart" for God

(e) Lesson in motives

2 Kin. 19:8–20

(a) Words/Action

(b) Prayer

(c) Results

(d) The "heart" for God

(e) Lesson in motives

 KINGDOM EXTRA

Using a Bible dictionary or encyclopedia, look up background information on how battles were generally fought in ancient times (for example, Babylonian, Persian, Greek, or Roman military warfare). See what principles of military strategy may teach us when applied to spiritual warfare. This can be a very profitable time of investigation, providing you with a useful instrument for sharing these truths with other Christians.

PROPER DISCIPLINE WINS BATTLES

The plight of an army who does not prepare for battle was clearly described at the beginning of this lesson. There is little hope for such a band of warriors when they encounter battle. Their only hope is if their opponents were even less diligent to prepare. But that will never be the case for us, for in the warfare that Christians fight, the enemy is constantly on the alert. How does 1 Peter 5:8 describe his readiness? What does Ephesians 6:11 say about his planning (look up "wiles")?

Because of these facts, it is imperative for us to be in a constant state of preparedness. Discipline is the key to our being ready for action. Just as with every area of life, when discipline is not maintained—physically, mentally, or spiritually—there comes an inevitable unavailability for effective action in the intended pursuit.

Below are scriptures that relate to Christian discipline. Some give directions for godly living and tell the blessings of walking righteously, while others tell the ramifications of not doing so. Summarize what is said about how believers are to live and note how you see that relating to victory in the battles you face.

Deut. 6:1–7, 17–19

Hebrews 10:19–25

1 John 3:18–23

 FAITH ALIVE

Have you ever thought of prayer as a means of "warring" unto the uplifting or defending of God's honor? What are your thoughts and feelings about this?

Do you desire to see God receive the glory for the things you do? Take time to confess to the Lord anything He brings to your mind right now of times when you have tried to keep the glory for yourself instead of giving the credit to Him.

Describe what you can do to grow as a person whose heart is set on seeing God glorified in every situation. Ask the Holy Spirit to show you new ways to bring glory to the Father.

List some of the specific ways in which you feel the Lord is calling you to be more disciplined.

Pray and ask the Holy Spirit to develop these areas of discipline in your life. The result should be a more joyful, freeing, and victorious life-style.

In making such analyses and self-assessments, remember that we are not attempting to establish superior righteousness but to accept the disciplines of a warrior. It is sometimes difficult to walk in basic Christian disciplines without becoming rigid and legalistic. If you find yourself feeling "trapped" to a set of rules, you're probably trying to do more than God has truly called you to right now, and are therefore attempting to do these things in your own strength instead of God's. If this is happening to you, ask someone with godly wisdom to help you prioritize which disciplines to start with, and allow the Lord to help you grow in those areas first before tackling the rest. Don't be discouraged or get caught in the trap of comparing yourself to others. Remember, well-discipled Christian warriors don't just happen. These areas of disciplines are ones we will continue to grow in throughout our lives.

OVERCOMERS IN HIS NAME

Jesus has called you to function *in His name*. This means that His power and authority are at your disposal to use. There is nothing that can overcome you as you walk in this power. This great blessing and awesome responsibility that Christ has given to us is rooted in the fact that to be sent "in His name" is to be delegated (a) as a fully authorized representative of Him, (b) with a full enduement of authority and power given for action. This blessing is mighty. We have all the power we will ever need to live a victorious Christian life and to be triumphant in conflict. There is nothing that can ultimately stop us, no power that can overcome us as we use His name with authority. This does not mean some battles will not be long, hard, and attended by sacrifice; but we will win! So, you may ask, why are some believers not living in this power? And what is lacking when people invoke Jesus' name and get no response?

This is where the responsibility of His name must be understood. If you are to exercise authority in His name, you must first be in submission to Him yourself. When an ambassador speaks on behalf of his country, he speaks the will of his nation, not his own. When you speak in Jesus' name, you must be speaking Jesus' will. If you try to function with your own will, then the right of His name is not yours to use.

Remember that Jesus said, "Not everyone who says to me, 'Lord, Lord,' shall enter the kingdom of heaven, but he who does the will of My Father in heaven" (Matt. 7:21). The issue is who will truly make Him Lord of their lives. These are the ones who live in submission to Him and can apply His name with authority and power.

What are ways "self-will" might hinder your power in prayer?

Here are some Bible references to help understand the power of Jesus' name. Through His name we are given all of the authority that He has been given. From the texts, write down the basis of your delegated authority as you discover it being expressed by Jesus Himself or as described by other writers.

Matt. 28:18

Luke 9:1

1 Cor. 15:27, 28

1 Pet. 3:22

 FAITH ALIVE

What does it mean to you personally that Jesus gave you the right to use His name? Write here a letter of response to Jesus. Express your feelings at having been entrusted with this privilege.

Does the fact of Christ's conferring His name upon you make you feel closer to Him? What else have you seen in this lesson that draws you nearer to Jesus?

What would you say is the most important point in facing spiritual battle? What makes this so vital?

What have you learned in this lesson that will help you in the situations you are already involved in? How do you see it helping? How will you put these things into action?

What areas of discipline for spiritual warfare do you need the Lord to help you grow in? Write these down as a prayer reminder and lay them before the Lord daily as you array for battle.

1. *Spirit-Filled Life Bible* (Nashville, TN: Thomas Nelson Publishers, 1991), 1267, "Word Wealth: 9:8 watchman."

Lesson 10/Fasting with Prayer

Were you ever frustrated as a child with the things that you had to do but didn't want to? I remember well the nights that I didn't want to go to bed, the days when I had no desire to go to school, the times when I would have gladly gone without a bath, haircut, nap time, or any one of the myriad of other childhood "problems" that were cast upon me by my parents. So it is with the mind of a child, with one too young to understand his or her own needs.

Paul mentions this way of thinking in 1 Corinthians 13:11. He explains that we once thought as children, but there is to be a different mind-set as we move toward maturity. As we mature, we begin to understand God's thinking compared with or in contrast to our own. By reason of our finiteness, next to the wisdom of God, our minds will always be as those of children, even as we mature. So it should come as no surprise to us that some of the things the Lord calls us to do not "compute" in our mode of thinking.

Fasting is one of these things. Some even question the place or validity of fasting. What did Jesus say? While Jesus may not have made a direct commandment, "Thou shalt fast!" He did make strong statements about fasting—words that cannot be circumvented and we dare not overlook as spiritual warriors.

To understand Jesus' call to fast, use the cited verses to answer these questions.

What does Jesus say in Mark 2:18–20 about His disciples fasting? What time does He say His disciples will fast?

What words of Jesus open His discourse on fasting in Matthew 6:16–18? What does this assume about His disciples?

Read the episode in Mark 9:14–29. From Jesus' concluding words, what can we learn about the power of fasting in certain cases?

FOR THOUGHTFUL CONSIDERATION

Some translations omit the words "and fasting" from Mark 9:29 and Matthew 17:21, even though as much manuscript evidence argues for their inclusion as for their omission as a later addition to the text. What reasons do you think might have motivated scholars to choose the option of omission, when inclusion is equally viable on all academic terms?

 ## WORD WEALTH

Fast, *tsom.* A fast; a day of fasting; a time set aside to mourn or pray with no provision for one's normal food needs. This noun comes from the verb *tsum,* "to fast." The verb occurs twenty-two times and the noun twenty-six times in the Old Testament. Fasting is a voluntary denial of food. The verb "fast" is sometimes coupled with the words "weep," "mourn," or "lay in sackcloth," all expressing intensity. Fasting is an action contrary to the first act of sin in the human race, which was eating what was forbidden. Fasting is refusing to eat what is allowed.[1]

Disciples, *matthetes.* From the verb *manthano,* "to learn," whose root *math* suggests thought with effort put forth. A disciple is a learner, one who follows both the teaching and the teacher. The word is used first of the Twelve and later of Christians generally, as in Acts 6:1. Because of this we understand that Jesus' directives to His disciples include all believers.[2]

    FAITH ALIVE

As you begin to look at fasting as it relates to spiritual warfare, take a few moments to prepare your thoughts. Review your past experiences with fasting and your inner feelings about it. Think through these questions and record your current views.

Do you ever fast? If so, when and why do you fast?

What is the hardest part for you when you fast? How do you, how have you, or how might you overcome this?

What has been your view of fasting in the past? What is it for? Present a biblical case for its importance and relevance today.

What do you think is the reason that Jesus suggests His disciples will fast in such times as ours?

FASTING IN THE EARLY CHURCH

It is clear from the statements of Jesus that His disciples are to be fasting now that He is not present on the earth in the physical form of His Incarnation. It is also obvious that the practice of fasting cannot be a 100%-of-the-time activity. The needs of our physical bodies are not unregarded by our Creator—ever! So, in order to see fasting in a balanced perspective, look through these scriptures to see how fasting was implemented and taught by Jesus' disciples in the early church.

Use these questions to guide you as you read these passages: What was the daily norm for the partaking of food in the early church? How was the practice of fasting seen? What was taught about fasting? How does this provide a balanced view of fasting?

Acts 2:42–46

Acts 6:1–7

Acts 10:2–4, 30, 31

Acts 14:23

Acts 27:21–26

2 Cor. 6:5; 11:27

BEHIND THE SCENES

While it was only required of the Jewish people to fast one day each year, on the Day of Atonement (Lev. 16:29), it had become the practice of the Pharisees to fast twice each week, Monday and Thursday. These were the market days in Jerusalem when those who put on the haggard face of fasting would be most noticed.

It was this appearance "to men to be fasting" that Jesus condemns in Matthew 6:16–18. On the contrary, Jesus' disciples are called to fast without putting on the affectations of the Pharisees.

In the early church the pattern of fasting twice each week, generally Wednesday and Friday, was common among believers. This was the beginning of the traditional church practice of fasting on Wednesday and Friday, a tradition mandated in parts of the church until more recent years.

God's mandatory fast for Israel, in Leviticus 16:29–34, introduces some patterns for understanding fasting in our personal life. ("Afflict your souls" is another expression for fasting.) What kinds of things does this Leviticus passage associate with fasting?

From Jesus' references to fasting in Mark 9:17–29 and Matthew 17:14–21, it is assumed that He practiced some regular pattern of fasting that exceeded His disciples' practice of keeping the annual fasts. What might this fact, along with the practice of patterned fasting in the early church, recommend to believers today?

WHEN FASTING BECOMES OUR RESPONSE

Most New Testament believers will acknowledge that fasting has some place in the church today, but few understand it. Just as with "spiritual warfare," which many neglect for want of teaching, so fasting—a powerful weapon in warfare—is overlooked. Still, even when fasting is believed and received as a potential periodic discipline, when some are asked, "When do you fast?" a common answer is, "Whenever the Holy Spirit prompts me to." That is not entirely unworthy as an answer, but there might be a need for addressing a deeper issue: *pattern* fasting. That is, might we look at more regular seasons of "planned" fasts? First, because Jesus already has told us to fast; and second, because it is inconsistent with the biblical examples of fasting to wait for a direct command from God to fast. Perhaps it should be noted that the Holy Spirit may issue such a directive if He desires to call an individual to a special fast for a specific purpose. But might we also agree that these should not be the sole times of fasting for the believer?

By using the scriptures below, see what you discover about why and when believers of Bible times fasted. Try to identify in each example: 1) the *purpose* of the fast; 2) the *decision* regarding the fast (who decided to fast and how did they make that decision); and 3) the *result* of the fast.

2 Sam. 12:15–24

Purpose *David's child*

Decision *No food pleaded with God for the child.*

Result *child died*

2 Chr. 20:1–24

Purpose

Decision

Result

Ezra 8:21–23, 31

Purpose

Decision

Result

Neh. 9:1–3; 10:28, 29

Purpose

Decision

Result

Dan. 6:6–28

Purpose

Decision

Result

Jon. 3:4–10

Purpose

Decision

Result

Luke 2:36–38

Purpose

Decision

Result

FAITH ALIVE

How do you feel about fasting after reading these passages? Have you seen anything so far in this lesson that gives you a greater desire to fast?

Time and time again believers in the Bible responded to needs by seeking God with fasting and prayer. How do you respond to such needs in your own life?

Do some situations require fasting and not others? Why do you think this is so? In what situations do you think fasting should be the response of every believer?

GOD'S WORD ON FASTING

Fasting is one discipline about which most Christians seem to understand the least. God has spoken a good deal about fasting in His Word, but few people take the time to search the Scriptures and learn about this powerful part of our spiritual life.

Use the following scriptures to learn more about fasting and the role that it takes in our spiritual walk. As you read through these passages, write down what points you are learning about fasting.

The fast God chooses: Is. 58:6–12

Record here what is said about the time, purpose, and power of fasting from God's perspective:

Time (v. 6a)

Purpose (vv. 6b, 7—note 8 things)

Power (vv. 8–12—note promises of results)

The opening five verses of Isaiah 58 were an attack on dead traditionalists who ritualized "fasts" but did not put their heart into it—only forms were observed. What lessons might be listed from that text?

How do Jesus' words on fasting in Matthew 6:16–18 coincide with what you have just read?

Different types of fasting:

Note from these texts different methods and lengths of fasting. List how long the fast was, what was consumed, and what their physical actions were.

Judg. 20:26

1 Chr. 10:11, 12

Esth. 4:15–17

Dan. 10:2, 3

Matt. 4:1, 2

FASTING: KEY TO BREAKTHROUGH

Although there is no one key to every solution except to do God's will, there are definite benefits in fasting. Power is released and breakthrough comes when God's people dedicate themselves to fasting and prayer. Many have come to love fasting, not because of the physical discipline, but because of the results seen in the spiritual realm when they fast.

In the scriptures listed below there are references to fasting and the results that came when God's people fasted. Read through these texts and answer the questions in order to learn more about this mighty tool of spiritual warfare.

Esth. 4:3, 16: What caused the Jewish people to fast?

Esther 9:1, 2 records the results of the Jews' fast. How does this contrast with the original decree placed against them in Esther 3:13?

Mark 9:17–29: What does Jesus say here about the unique power of fasting?

How is this also related to faith in the story?

 ## FAITH ALIVE

Now that you have completed this lesson on fasting, use this section to help you reflect on the things you have learned.

What stands out to you as the most notable thing about fasting? Do you see this being practiced in your own life? How?

Describe whatever pattern of fasting you have kept in the past. Do you feel that this is a healthy or unhealthy pattern? Explain.

What changes or truths will affect your pattern of fasting as a result of this lesson?

Why do you think Jesus so strongly encouraged faith in a situation that required fasting and prayer? Could it be that the faith needed here was developed through fasting?

As you conclude, take a few minutes to pray over your answers here. Ask the Lord to give you the strength you need as you grow in this discipline of warfare in your life.

1. *Spirit-Filled Life Bible* (Nashville, TN: Thomas Nelson Publishers, 1991), 1314, "Word Wealth: 3:5 fast."

2. Ibid., 1421, "Word Wealth: 10:1 disciples."

Lesson 11/Actions in Battle

Have you ever noticed that baseball batters tap their bats on home plate as they take their stance? Have you ever asked yourself, "What does this have to with baseball? Is the batter proving he knows where the plate is? Could it be the plate would move itself from the playing field if it were not constantly pounded into the ground?" Nonsense! Of course, neither of these ideas is proposed by anyone. Still, it's true that during any baseball game, this strange practice continues—the plate is "assaulted" by numerous clubs as players take their turn at bat.

I never really thought much about this practice—took it for granted as we all do—until my small son got his first baseball bat. Before long, it was being pommeled against the asphalt by another boy playing street ball, almost shredding the end of the bat. That prompted concern—-the bat cost 15 bucks! But out of curiosity, I asked the little boy why he was pounding the bat on the pavement. The child's reply was simply: "That's what the big league players do before they hit the ball!" It seemed obvious to him: the plate must be struck if the batter is going to hit the ball!

While somewhere in the beginning days of baseball there may have been a reason for establishing this universal ritual, it clearly has nothing essential to do with hitting the ball. And in review, one asks: "What motions might Christians go through that are not to the point?" What actions are essential? Which are superstitious? Are there practices that may seem superstitious or naive to some, but that *are* important? The answer is "yes." And further, if one has never been taught, or never taken time to learn, he or she may think that these actions are only rituals that have nothing to do with the actual work the Lord has assigned us. Even others may feel embarrassed by demonstrative actions of spiritual warfare and choose to deny a place for physical actions that push boundaries of pride or self-consciousness and crowd their comfort zones.

God has shown us actions that accompany spiritual warfare in His Word. These may set easily within or radically outside the boundaries of our own personal tastes, but they are set firmly within His plan for us. If there is stretching that needs to occur, it is always so that our boundaries will be expanded to allow us to grow to possess all that God has for us. Remember that we are learning about real warfare and not some symbolic contest. Battlefields are seldom "comfortable," but they are glorious in victory—and they are never without *action!*

It is both the understanding communication *and* the actions of the troops that bring victory in the battle. For in warfare these actions are directed by our Leader in battle—the Almighty Lord of Hosts. His Word records evidence of these actions and their application. Read through the scriptures provided to learn more about the value and place of physical actions in spiritual battle.

Ex. 17:8–16: What were the actions of Moses, Aaron, and Hur during the battle?

Describe the impact that Moses' actions had on the course of the battle.

Why were Aaron and Hur vital to the battle's being won?

What did Moses do after the fight in response to victory?

Judg. 6:24–40; 7:16–25: What two things does Gideon do as a statement of his commitment to follow God? (6:24–27)

In light of the trying times in which Gideon lived, how does he show his faith through the naming of the altar he builds?

What steps does Gideon pursue to verify the Lord's direction?

By what actions do the soldiers initiate battle?

Describe the results of the actions taken by the soldiers.

2 Kin. 19:8–19, 35–37: Describe how Hezekiah showed his distress to the Lord.

What did he symbolically do with Sennacherib's letter?

Explain what the Lord did to Sennacherib and his army.

 FAITH ALIVE

It is not always an easy thing to assimilate and apply the principles that are found in Scripture. Look over the instances that you just studied and use this section to help you apply them to your life.

When Moses was watching the children of Israel in battle in Exodus 17, he was located above the fighting on a hilltop in view of the army. Explain why it is important for you to see your position in Christ as being above the struggles of this world (Eph. 2:1–6).

Why do you think it could be important for an intercessor to see from the vantage point that Moses had? Why do you think it could be important for the people in battle to be able to see their intercessor as Moses was seen?

Both Gideon and Moses built and named altars unto the Lord. Likewise, it is important that we recognize the turning points in our lives by establishing a place—whether in physical dedication or in our memories—that we can return to in worship to thank the Lord for how He has directed us.

Describe one of these life-changing experiences—one that shaped the course of your life.

 KINGDOM EXTRA

Establish an "altar of remembrance" in your room—a commemoration of something the Lord has done. This could be as simple as a rock set by the fireplace, a photo album, a memento of an occasion of victory— something of special significance to you. Let this become a visible "testimony"—a praise point—so that each time you see it you will be reminded of God's special blessing, provision, or guidance in your life.

Whether in thanksgiving for what He has done or in anticipation for what He will do, take a *faith action* here and now. Inscribe on paper and make a simple scroll. Write down one area of your life in which you seek the Lord's goodness and help. Let this physical reminder be another "connecting point" between what you believe and what is yet invisible but being anticipated by faith.

(**Caution:** These actions are not superstitious substitutes for faith, but living, visible, praise-focused expressions of faith.)

USING GOD'S TRUMPET

It may seem surprising that one of the most enduring implements of military action is not aimed at the Adversary, but rather is directed toward one's own comrades. The trumpet has been used as an instrument of battle from ancient times and is still used as a signal today, though modern communications have replaced it in actual combat.

In Scripture the trumpet has a prominent place in spiritual warfare and conduct. Throughout the Old Testament the trumpet is used symbolically and literally to bring God's people to a new place, whether through military victory or daily pursuit of divine guidance.

In the "Word Wealth" section below are several descriptions of the trumpet as it was used in the Bible. Some passages refer to a literal trumpet and some are figurative expressions or means by which attention is gained and action directed.

 ### WORD WEALTH

Trumpet, *shophar.* A trumpet made from a curved animal horn; a cornet. The *shophar* is mentioned seventy-two times in the Old Testament and is used to herald the Lord's descent at the giving of the Law. It is also used to warn of danger and as a call to arms. In Hosea 8:1 *shophar* is compared to a prophet's voice which proclaims the word of God.[1]

Voice, *qol.* To call aloud, call out, a voice or sound. To proclaim, claim or thunder. The usage of *qol* in Isaiah 58:1 shows a definite call to proclaim loudly the word of the Lord. This is a physical action that requires volume in our voice.

Quiet, *shaquat.* To repose, appease, settle, be at rest. *Shaquat* carries the meaning of quietness of life and circumstance. After the battle there is a settled life of rest or freedom from upset and strife. (See 2 Chr. 20:30.)

Jubilee, *truwah.* Clamor, acclamation of joy, the battle cry, a sounding of trumpets. *Truwah* also denotes rejoicing, celebration, joy and jubilee. In Leviticus 25:9 the trumpets were sounded to indicate a time of great rejoicing and freedom throughout Israel. This was a celebration that happened once every fifty years and was a dedicated year of the returning of lost family inheritance to their intended owners. This portrays how Jesus' work on the Cross is meant to restore to us what God had intended for us.

Keeping these descriptions in mind, read the scriptures that follow and record the type of situation illustrated and the result of the trumpet's use. Write down any special insights that, as you study, seem to make a contemporary spiritual application to you.

Num. 10:1–10

Judg. 7:16–25

1 Sam. 13:3

1 Chr. 15:25

2 Chr. 20:27–30

Is. 58:1

Ezek. 3:10, 11

 FAITH ALIVE

The trumpet was used in biblical times to direct the movement of the troops in battle. With spiritual warfare, the Lord gives us a similar responsibility to "sound the trumpet" with our voices and, by His word, direct the battle according to His plan.

Are you ready to sound the trumpet in this way? Search your heart as you answer the following questions. Allow this self-evaluation to help you grow in your role as an intercessor.

Describe what you think the scripture means when it says to "lift up your voice like a trumpet" (Is. 58:1).

How does the past study on the use of trumpets in battle help you to see greater use for your voice in prayer warfare?

Perhaps the lack of some people to show balance and sensitivity in their openly verbal expressions of prayer has kept you from praying openly with passion. What can you do to help overcome the natural reticence to speak out your prayers with boldness?

What things do you plan on doing in the future to help you pray more boldly and confidently?

Because God has created us each as unique individuals, we will each function in different ways. Some people are naturally more demonstrative and more vocal than others, but still the Lord calls all of us to raise our voices before Him on certain occasions. At other times, He instructs us to be still in His presence. The key then is to be sensitive to His leading and live in a proper balance.

Stop now and take a moment to pray—and to openly, boldly, and verbally ask Him to refill you with His Spirit. Lift up praise as you welcome His enabling you to walk in a balanced, vibrantly victorious life.

PUTTING WEAPONS TO USE

Throughout the history of warfare there have been many weapons and tools used to wage contests. But the best preparation, training, and strategic maneuvering cannot win the fight unless the warrior effectively wields the implements of combat. Likewise, believers should not expect to see victory without participating in the physical actions of the battle.

The Lord calls us to be effective warriors in the battles that we face. As we accept our place in battle, it is important to be aware of the troop movements which are directed by our Commander in Chief. His directives may be specific or they may come as a natural response to situations as a result of our relationship with Him and our understanding of His methods. It is wise then to learn more about our physical actions of response and participation while on the battle line.

The Scriptures show us many physical elements to use in our spiritual campaign. Read the texts below and list some of these physical actions, describing the basic use of each "weapon" as it relates to spiritual warfare.

Josh. 6:2–5 (As you compare with Rom. 4:12 and Gen. 13:14–18, noting v. 17, what might be concluded as appropriate spiritual action to take today?)

Josh. 10:12, 13

2 Chr. 20:21, 22 (compare with Acts 16:16–26—v. 25)

Is. 58:1 (compare with Acts 4:24)

THE WARFARE OF WORSHIP

Worship is our most effective means of advance in any situation. Through worship, the presence of God and lordship of Christ is invited into your current circumstance. There is nothing more powerful than establishing this as a priority in your everyday life.

The Bible shows that many actions associated with worship are also seen in battle. This emphasizes the place of worship in warfare, as well as showing still more of God's designs for our movement in combat.

Continue with the scriptures below as you did in the preceding section, listing and describing the actions and weapons of spiritual warfare.

Ps. 47:1–3

Ps. 100:1–5

Ps. 150:4

 FAITH ALIVE

Take some time to review your work on this lesson. There is so much to learn about spiritual warfare and the weapons that we wield as we are engaged in battle. No one lesson or even complete set of lessons will teach you all that there is to know, but be assured that the Lord knows what you need to prepare you for each situation you encounter.

1. *Spirit-Filled Life Bible* (Nashville, TN: Thomas Nelson Publishers, 1991), 1266, "Word Wealth: 8:1 trumpet."

Lesson 12/Angelic Ministers

When I was a young boy, my least favorite part of visiting with my grandparents was that my brother and I always slept in the basement. Although this basement was large, paved, and had long before been converted into use as an everyday part of the house, it still seemed a universe away from the upstairs rooms where the rest of the family stayed. As the youngest boy, I was always the first one in bed, and I remember being especially afraid one particular night.

My grandmother had come to tuck me in, and I knew that soon she would go back upstairs and leave me alone to go to bed. I was afraid to be alone. Though no one knew it, and I didn't say so, I felt isolated in this remote corner of the world where darkness and the sounds of an old house would be my sole company until I finally fell asleep. Even the night-light was not enough to make me feel secure.

And so it was until this special night, when my grandmother shared with me a testimony of the way the angels of God are sent to protect us. She told of an occasion when one of our family had their spiritual eyes opened to see an angel standing watch over their home. I knew the promise of Psalm 91:9–12, but I was deeply moved by the present-day testimony. I still recall that story and how it served to alleviate my fears for many nights to come. I felt safe to be alone as I drifted off to sleep, because I knew that God's angels were truly there—as promised—to protect me.

Over the years I have heard many accounts from believers who have seen or been made aware of angels assisting, encouraging, and protecting them in times of trouble, as well as in day-to-day life. These narratives seem to stir up interest among Christians today as they remind many that angels are as real and active now as they were in ancient times. Often the relating of current and personal events tend to impact us more than the hearing of long past occurrences with which we have no personal experience.

As you begin this study of angels, keep in mind that the things you read about in the Bible are just as true today as they were then. Angels are present, ministering today just as surely as they have been since God created them.

In Psalm 103:20, 21 reference is made to five ministries of angels which are listed below. As you read through the following scripture verses, note any other descriptions of angelic activity that are given, such as methods of angelic work, angelic appearance, specific and general names used when referring to angels, and so on.

"Bless the Lord"

Neh. 9:6

Heb. 1:6

"Do His word"

Matt. 13:41, 42

Matt. 26:52–54

"Heeding the voice of [God's] word"

Dan. 9:21–23; 10:5–14

Luke 1:26–38

"Ministers" on His behalf

1 Kin. 19:5–8

Heb. 1:13, 14

"Do His pleasure"

Luke 16:22

Acts 12:5–11

FAITH ALIVE

Before you proceed with this study, stop and answer the following questions to help you establish your beliefs regarding angels. Pray and ask the Lord to help you see the complete truth about these beings of His creation and how they impact your life.

What stories or testimonies do you remember hearing about angels? Were those stories fiction or nonfiction, simple or complex, exciting or mundane? Describe them briefly.

How do you think these stories have shaped your understanding of angels and what they do?

How might a biblical perception of angels affect your life?

Have you gained any new insights about the angelic realm from this portion of our study? Has your viewpoint changed in any way? What practical applications can you see in this subject as it bears on spiritual warfare?

THE MINISTRY OF ANGELS TOWARD GOD'S PEOPLE

Throughout the Bible, it is made clear that God's people are called to serve one another. Each of us is called to serve God's family in our service to the Lord. As parents serve the needs of their newborn baby, providing the care and nurturing that is required without being controlled by the child, so as servants in the body of Christ, we are not assigned to be under the control of those we serve. Rather, we choose to serve one another, as a way of ministering to the Lord.

In the same way, angels are in the direct service of our Heavenly Father. They will do nothing that is not ordained of God. However, in their service to God, they serve His people on His behalf, and, as they do, it is important to remember that although they serve us, they are not subject to our control.

Some believers have misunderstood this, having heard another believer "command" an angel to act. But while a situation may appear as though a Christian "commanded an angel to act," the Bible teaches us that angels will only perform what is directed from God. Therefore, we can know that, in those cases where we see angels operating in response to man's prayers, the words spoken were not the will of man, but actually a reflection of God's word for that specific instance. God *does* use His people to speak forth His word, and when we speak out in accordance with His will, His ministering angels will respond. Thus we understand that we do not control angels, but we have been invited to partner with the Lord in prayer and warfare—to advance the accomplishing of His will—His kingdom expanding its dominion "on earth as in heaven."

Keeping these things in mind, use the scriptures below to list and define some of the ministries that angels render toward us as God's people. As the Lord of Hosts, He directs them to move beside us in the conflict. See how they take action.

Ps. 34:7; Luke 4:10, 11

Luke 16:22

Luke 22:43

Acts 8:26

Gal. 1:8

Heb. 1:14

 FAITH ALIVE

Very few things become vital parts of our lives unless we are able to define them in our own words and experience. Take a moment to review the things that you have studied in this last section and think about how they impact you personally. Use the questions in this section to help you establish the truths that you have learned in your own life.

What part of the angels' assistance to believers seems most pertinent to you? How do you expect your life to be benefited by this work?

How does it affect you to know that God appoints His angels to minister to you? Describe what you see of God's heart for you demonstrated by this fact.

Write in your own words a note of thanks to God for His care for you. Express your feelings to the Lord concerning the angelic beings that He has appointed to minister to you. Thank Him also for the things that you anticipate in the future because of His provision for you.

ANGELS AND SPIRITUAL WARFARE

Any study of the work of angels would not be complete without considering the spiritual realm and seeing the impact that angels have in spiritual warfare. Scripture makes it clear that angels have positions of spiritual power that affect the course of nations and peoples.

In this section we will be focusing on the actions of angels impacting warfare in the invisible realm. Use the questions provided to help you discover the work of the heavenly hosts in battle and how it relates to what you do.

Rev. 12:7–11: As the battle is joined to throw Satan out of heaven, who are the primary combatants?

Describe the result of this warfare.

What are the means used to cast Satan out of heaven?

List the names used in this passage to denote Satan.

What is sealed for you as a result of this victory?

What is the means by which the saints overcome?

Dan. 10:1–4, 12, 13: What was Daniel's place in the warfare mentioned here?

How did he live out this responsibility?

When was the angel sent to Daniel? What was it that detained him?

What happened to allow this angel the freedom to continue with his mission toward Daniel?

What other spiritual beings are mentioned here, and how are they described?

What place of power is related to angelic beings in this text? Relate that to the order of spiritual beings listed in Ephesians 6:12.

 FAITH ALIVE

Now that you have seen what the Scripture tells us about the work and ministry of angels, reflect upon the things that you have discovered. Use the questions listed here to help you think about what this lesson has revealed and how you can apply this truth to your daily life.

How does the knowledge of the work of angels in spiritual warfare influence your approach to spiritual battle?

As we discern more of the Lord's plans and working in our lives, we sometimes see how God was at work in past events in ways that we never saw at the time. In what ways have you seen the things learned here already at work in your life?

What are some things that you expect to see happen in your life as a result of new insights you have received from this study?

Lesson 13/Angels and Demons

As I walked into the room, I could see angels everywhere I looked. It seemed that every available space had its own angelic representation. No, this was not some super-spiritual vision; it was simply the items that composed the room's decoration. It was Christmas—and obviously at this festive time, angels had been chosen as the motif of decor in this chamber of the house.

It is not uncommon during the Yuletide season to see such holiday decorations. It is in every way appropriate that we, who have received such a wonderful salvation, should celebrate with joy the birth of our Savior. And further, it's fully acceptable to employ the ornaments we use to reflect the Christmas story in many ways: nativity scenes remind us of the birth of Christ; lights that adorn buildings and homes remind us that the Light of the world has come.

The beauty of His gift to us is radiated in the magnificence that surrounds our celebration of Jesus' birth. Amid it all are angels—angels of every description—which abound in memory of those angelic hosts who first *proclaimed* to the shepherds the good tidings of the Savior's birth, and who *protected* Him when Herod became the instrument of the Adversary's attack (Luke 2:8–14; Matt. 2:13).

Christmas is one time when we think about angels. But there are other occasions when popular opinion about angels is often stated: "What an angelic child!" is spoken about a sleeping infant whose face portrays such peacefulness. Someone else will refer to the full-cheeked face of a toddler as being "like a little cherub," and the best child in the Sunday School class is said to have "behaved just like an angel."

These are phrases that most of us have heard or even spoken ourselves, but does anyone really know what angels look like or act like? Is there one "angelic" look that truly resembles the heavenly host? Are angels indeed always surrounded by peacefulness?

Angels have been characterized in so many ways and have come to symbolize various things to different people. Some of these ideas are based on biblical record and some on artistic or creative thought. The result has been a hodgepodge of myths and speculation, confusing many Christians' minds about the sphere of the angelic.

To begin researching the biblical facts about angels, read through the following scriptures and list the types of angels described.

Gen. 3:24

Judg. 13:3

Is. 6:2

1 Thess. 4:16

1 Pet. 3:22

Rev. 12:7–9

 WORD WEALTH

Angel, *malach.* A messenger, ambassador; someone dispatched to do a task or relay a message; specifically an "angel" or heavenly messenger from the Lord. *Malach* is used more than two hundred times in the Old Testament and is usually translated "angel." This word can be used of humans, in which case it is generally translated "messenger." Angels, mentioned extensively in the Old Testament, were sent to assist or inform the patriarchs, Balaam, David, the prophet Zechariah, and others. Not all angels are the "angelic" sort; see Proverbs 16:14 (which might have been translated "death angels"). The supernatural qualities of the Lord's messengers are portrayed in Psalms 78:49; 104:4, and Proverbs 17:11.[1]

Angels, *angelos.* From *angello,* "to deliver a message"; hence, a messenger. In the New Testament the word has a special sense of a spiritual, heavenly personage attendant upon God and functioning as a messenger from the Lord sent to earth to execute His purposes and make them known to men. Angels are invisibly present in the assemblies of Christians and are appointed by God to minister to believers (Heb. 1:14).[2]

THE ANGEL OF THE LORD

In the Old Testament the term "the Angel of the Lord" is used on various occasions. Some believe this refers to a preincarnate visitation of Jesus, while others maintain that it is no different from any other angel. Look deeper into this issue and see what you can learn about the Angel of the Lord.

Below are some of the scriptures that relate to the Angel of the Lord and to other angelic visitations. Use the questions below to help you evaluate and compare these texts.

Does the Angel of the Lord accept worship?

Do other angels accept worship?

What is the appearance of the Angel of the Lord?

How does the Lord appear in physical form in the Old Testament?

What other terms are used to describe the Angel of the Lord?

Gen. 18:1–33

Gen. 48:15, 16

Ex. 3:2–8

Josh. 5:13–15

Judg. 13:3–6

Rev. 19:10; 22:8, 9

FAITH ALIVE

Virtually all evangelical scholars agree that the Angel of the Lord who appears in the Old Testament is, in fact, Jesus. We have just studied some of the numerous reasons to believe this, but none is more convincing than the undeniable fact that Jesus is central to the entire Bible.

Now that you have done your own study into the Angel of the Lord, think about what you have learned and how that impacts you. How does it feel to think of Old Testament figures speaking to Jesus face-to-face?

How does knowing that Jesus was directly involved with Old Testament events affect your thoughts about God's workings among the people of that time?

Does it make the event seem any more or less appropriate as a living example for your life today? How?

When you see clearly that Jesus has always been involved in God's workings with men, His presence can be felt as more immediate and expected rather than aloof and sporadic. Knowing that He is right here and involved with you, ask Jesus to help you see Him more clearly in your daily life.

CHARACTERISTICS AND TYPES OF ANGELS

Of the various types of angels mentioned in the Bible, the cherubim and the seraphim are probably the most distinct. Use the scripture texts below to form a composite idea of what these angelic creatures are like. As you record your findings, look for descriptions of their appearance and work. Also look at the Word Wealth section to help you in your research.

<u>Cherubim</u>

Gen. 3:24

Ex. 25:18–22

Ex. 37:7–9

Ps. 99:1

Ezek. 10:1–22

<u>Seraphim</u>

Isaiah 6:2, 3

Is. 6:6, 7

WORD WEALTH

Cherubim, *keruvim.* A heavenly being represented by carved gold figures on the ark of the covenant. *Keruv* may be related to an Akkadian verb meaning, "to bless, praise, adore." *Keruvim* are mentioned ninety times in the Old Testament, more than thirty of these references being in Ezekiel. *Keruvim* were observed from Adam's time to Ezekiel's time and are described in Ezekiel 10. The idea persists that *keruv* means "covering angel" (Ezek. 28:14). A *keruv* does cover, as Exodus 25:20 states. (Compare the two angels facing each other, who covered and guarded the Lord of Glory, as His body lay quietly in death, John 20:12.)[3]

Seraphim, *seraphim*, plural of *seraph.* A burning, fiery, gliding, angelic being; also a fire-colored, agile, gliding desert creature, presumably a fiery serpent. The root is the verb *seraph,* "to set on fire, to burn." Accordingly, the *seraphim* may be angels of a fiery color or appearance, or flamelike in motion or clearness. Only in Isaiah 6:2, 6 does the word appear as "seraphim"; in all the remaining five occurrences (Num. 21:6, 8; Deut. 8:15; Is. 14:29; 30:6), it is translated "fiery serpents" and appears along with scorpions and vipers. Perhaps the color of motion of the earthly fiery serpents resembles that of the fiery angels.[4]

KINGDOM EXTRA

Angels are mentioned throughout the entire Bible. They perform many different tasks, appear in different forms, and arrive different ways. Using a concordance or topical Bible, form a comparison report of angelic activities. This can help you to gain a greater understanding of their purpose and work. You may want to report any or all of the following details that the scripture provides for the angels in each situation.

Appearance	Words spoken	Method of movement
Name	Type of angel	Angel's purpose
Actions	Clothing	Introduction

There may also be other things about these situations that you would choose to note. Feel free to add to this list and write special comments as you go.

Scripture mentions that there is a definite order of authority among the angelic host, though it does not define these positions clearly in most situations. What you will be studying here are creatures that are simply called angels along with the most exalted of these beings known as an "archangel." Nothing is said to indicate that the archangel's appearance and duties differ from those of the lesser angels except that he is recognized as a leader among them.

With this in mind, look into the description of angels found in the Scripture. Remember to record what you see about their appearance and specific duties.

<u>Archangels</u>

Dan. 10:12, 13, 20, 21

1 Thess. 4:16

Jude 9

<u>Angels, Heavenly Host</u>

Gen. 19:1–5

Ps. 91:11

Ps. 104:4

Ps. 148:2

Luke 1:11–20

Luke 2:9–15

 ## FAITH ALIVE

After looking through these scriptures above, what is your impression of the various angels?

What things have you learned about angels that have been surprising to you?

What do you think is the most important thing that you have learned in this lesson? Why do you feel this is more important than other things you have found?

Write down several things you have learned that you think will have a continuing impact on your life. Pray over these things and ask the Lord to help you live in what He is teaching you.

THE FALLEN ANGELS

Isaiah 14:12–14 tells the story of Lucifer, who was once an angel of the Lord, being cast out of heaven because of His sin. We now know this fallen angel as Satan, as he has lost his right to his original God-given name as well as his place in heaven.

When Satan was expelled from heaven, a number of other angels who had followed his rebellion were cast out also. It is generally accepted that these fallen angels are now the demonic forces of hell that we combat. This line of thought is based on the fact that Satan cannot create, and therefore demons must be the fallen state of some divinely created beings. Although this idea is not directly stated, it is supported in Scripture (Rev. 12:9).

The key thing to remember as you study this topic is that we have authority over these fallen angels in Jesus' name. Use the references listed below to see what is said about fallen angels and their current standing as it relates to us.

Is. 14:12–15

Matt. 25:41

Mark 16:17, 18

Rom. 8:38, 39

Eph. 1:20–22

Rev. 12:7–10

 FAITH ALIVE

Talking about the demonic realm can be a frightening thing to those who do not understand our place in Christ. Explain what authority Jesus has given you over demons.

Often when Christians first begin to understand the authority we have in Jesus' name, they may become overly excited about dealing with the demonic. What do you think will keep your life in balance in this area? (See Luke 10:17–20.)

As you have worked through this lesson, are there any things you have learned that you had not known before? What are they?

What steps will you take to establish these truths into your life this next week?

Take a moment as you conclude to write a letter of thanks to the Lord for the things in this lesson you have seen of His majesty. You may want to include thanks for angels that He has appointed to minister to you and the authority over the works of darkness that are yours through Jesus.

1. *Spirit-Filled Life Bible* (Nashville, TN: Thomas Nelson Publishers, 1991), 647, "Word Wealth: 37:21 angel."

2. Ibid., 1409, "Word Wealth: 4:11 angels."

3. Ibid., 118, "Word Wealth: 25:18 cherubim."

4. Ibid., 69, "Word Wealth: 6:2 seraphim."

A Summary and Postlude:
The Whole Picture

The last two lessons have directed your attention to the characteristics of real, active beings in the spiritual realm. We have examined these not for idle fascination or curiosity about angels, but because of the impact that these beings have on the outcome of our prayers and the whole spiritual conflict. There is probably not a battle we face or a victory we gain as believers, but that somehow, beyond our vision, the ministering work of angels is involved. The evidence of scripture is that they are accompanying us as we go, focused in faith and battle.

These chapters have been included to help you better understand the arena in which you function as a believer in Jesus. As you work through this final section, look at how God's Word knits it together with our earlier focus on prayer and spiritual warfare, introducing the matter of angels into this full, powerful picture of our place as servant-soldiers in the kingdom of God.

Work step-by-step through Ephesians 6:10–18, adding your own notes to the commentary provided. Be especially aware of how the three major themes of this study guide are presented in harmony. Note that the importance of each is emphasized without overshadowing or negating any of the need for the others.

Ephesians 6:10–18

Verse 10: This is an injunction to place all of our dependence on the Lord. There is no place in a Christian's life for a dependence on our own strength. Indeed, leaning on one's own power is a sign of spiritual weakness, not strength. His strength is made available to every believer through prayer.

Where is the Lord most calling you to give up your strength for His—calling you to a new, deepened dependence on His grace and power at distinct points in your life?

Verse 11: Coming to Him in prayer is only the beginning of walking in His strength. This verse calls us to take an aggressive stance in spiritual warfare. More than prayers alone, spiritual warfare recognizes that there is a strategy involved. The tactics (wiles) of the Devil are calculated plans to bring the downfall of God's kingdom. We are called to uphold and extend His kingdom through a strategy for battle set out by our Lord. Here is where warfare surpasses prayer, in that it presents a strategy for victory, not just a report of circumstance.

What strategies are you perceiving the Lord seeking to work in your prayer life? Can you see how He's pointing to an ultimate plan for victory? Describe what you see.

Verse 12: We do not contend in the physical realm, facing some enemy of flesh and blood, but our battle is in the spiritual realm. Our enemy is to be understood as being of the unseen spiritual world. It is therefore vital to gain some understanding of authority in this arena.

NOTE: This verse spells out a picture of levels of spiritual authority. The terms "principalities," "powers," "rulers of darkness of this age," and "spiritual *hosts* of wickedness in *heavenly* places" are all terms denoting different placements of spiritual oversight and authority. These terms range from one who would have mastery over a single person, or group of people, to a depiction of Satan as being over all evil upon the earth. They are provided to affirm that we need to be prepared to contend with some greater and some lesser entities as we fight the foe. It is folly to think every demon or hellish power is of the same strength, as it will lead us to be ill-prepared for battles we will face.

Ask the Lord to show you ways you tend to deal more with "flesh and blood" enemies, rather than dealing with the evil principalities motivating human sinning, rebellion, immorality and political confusion, corruption or war. How should this insight translate into balanced behavior—with social sensitivity and action joined to discerning prayer and passionate, intercessory warfare?

Verses 13–17: Again, we are instructed to take up what the Lord has provided for our warfare. Not only is the strength His, but the weapons are also. Our own weapons and tactics will fail, but He has provided all that we need. Take all of His provision so that you will be found standing after the battle is done. This again requires our willingness to take (aggressively) and receive (willingly) the armor (clothing for battle) that the Lord provides. When we do this, we will be found standing when the battle is completed.

Lesson 7 provides an extensive look at each of the pieces of armor noted in these verses. Look at the chart provided with that lesson and review the value of the armor of God. Remember again, this is to protect every area of your life, but the armor will only work as a complete outfit.

Now, write a personal response to each piece of armor God offers—take it. Put it on as a distinct, prayerful action.

Verse 18: The conclusion of this passage is a call to prayer. The placement of this verse in the context makes clear that <u>the whole of our preparation and engagement of the battle happens through prayer.</u>

Summarize decisions you have been reaching in your whole study of this subject.

The areas of prayer, warfare, and the realities of the spiritual realm cannot be separated. To do so would so compromise the others as to render them ineffective. But in Christ, in His power and attending presence, it is possible to live in all that He has done for us as we accept His charge, take up His armor, and with prayer, assault the powers of darkness in the spiritual arena.

Rise, dear fellow-soldier!

Take this charge with you and believe, and watch as you grow to be a victorious warrior in God's army!